World's Greatest Collection of CLEAN J★KES

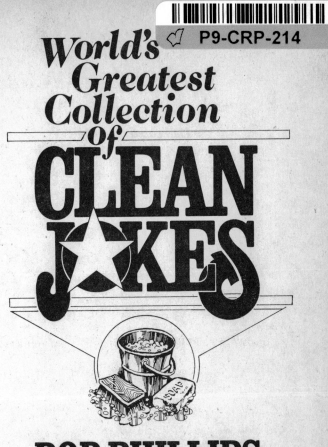

BOB PHILLIPS

HARVEST HOUSE PUBLISHERS
Eugene, Oregon 97402

*Dedicated to anyone
who buys my joke book*

THE WORLD'S GREATEST COLLECTION OF CLEAN JOKES

Copyright © 1974 Vision House Publishers
Published by Harvest House Publishers
Eugene, Oregon 97402

ISBN 0-89081-456-2

Printed in the U.S.A.

CONTENTS

INTRODUCTION

As one attempts to write a book, even a joke book, he often encounters periods of depression and a slowing of motivation. During periods of depression, I was spurred on by an important quote designed for writers:

> If you steal from one author, it's plagiarism;
>
> If you steal from two or three authors, it's literary discernment;
>
> If you steal from many, it's masterful research.

Joke telling can be a lot of fun. Or it can be disaster, like the man who told a joke and everyone booed except one man: he was applauding the booing.

If you would like to guarantee disaster in your joke telling, follow these suggestions:

1. Make sure you forget the punch line; sadists enjoy a letdown.

2. Laugh at your own joke and be sure to jab your audience during the process.

3. Tell the same story over if the point is missed. This will assure at least wry smiles.

4. Make sure the story is long enough to lull the dull ones to sleep.

5. Tell the wrong joke to the wrong audience; they'll feel worse than you do.

6. Above all else, don't be yourself, because you know you're not humorous even if you are funny.

If, on the other hand, you would like to have some measure of success in joke telling—ignore the above suggestions.

Bob Phillips

ADAM AND EVE

Q: "At what time of day was Adam born?"
A: "A little before Eve."

☆   ☆   ☆

What a good thing Adam had—when he said something he knew nobody had said it before.

☆   ☆   ☆

Q: "When was radio first mentioned in the Bible?"
A: "When the Lord took a rib from Adam and made a loud speaker."

☆   ☆   ☆

Eve: "Adam, do you love me?"
Adam: "Who else?"

☆   ☆   ☆

The first Adam-splitting gave us Eve, a force which ingenious men in all ages have never gotten under control.

☆   ☆   ☆

Adam and Eve were naming the animals of the earth when along came a rhinoceros.

Adam: "What shall we call this one?"

Eve: "Let's call it a rhinoceros."

Adam: "Why?"

Eve: "Well, it looks more like a rhinoceros than anything we've named yet."

☆   ☆   ☆

Adam was created first . . . to give him a chance to say something.

☆   ☆   ☆

Teacher: "Why was Adam a famous runner?"

Student: "Because he was first in the human race."

☆   ☆   ☆

AIRPLANES

A farmer and his wife went to a fair. The farmer was fascinated by the airplane rides, but he balked at the $10 tickets.

"Let's make a deal," said the pilot. "If you and your wife can ride without making a single sound, I won't charge you anything. Otherwise you pay the ten dollars."

"Good deal!" said the farmer.

So they went for a ride. When they got back the pilot said, "If I hadn't been there, I never would have believed it. You never made a sound!"

"It wasn't easy, either," said the farmer. "I almost yelled when my wife fell out."

☆ ☆ ☆

He: "Excuse me, stewardess. How high is this plane?"
She: "About thirty thousand feet."
He: "Oh; and how wide is it?"

☆ ☆ ☆

The loud speaker of the big jet clicked on and the captain's voice announced in a clear, even tone: "Now there's no cause for alarm but we felt you passengers should know that for the last three hours we've been flying without the benefit of radio-compass, radar, or navigational beam due to the breakdown of certain key components. This means that we are, in the broad sense of the word, lost and are not quite sure in which direction we are heading. I'm sure you'll be glad to know, however . . . on the brighter side of the picture . . . that we're making excellent time!"

☆ ☆ ☆

An airliner flew into a violent thunderstorm and was soon swaying and bumping around the sky. One very nervous lady happened to be sitting next to a clergyman and turned to him for comfort.

"Can't you do something?" she demanded force-fully.

"I'm sorry, ma'am," said the reverend gently. "I'm in sales, not management."

☆ ☆ ☆

A man is now able to go around the world in three

hours . . . one hour for flying, and the other two to get to the airport.

☆ ☆ ☆

The airline company was disturbed over a high percentage of accidents, and decided to eliminate human errors by building a completely mechanical plane.

"Ladies and gentlemen," came a voice over a loud speaker on the maiden voyage, "it may interest you to know that you are now traveling in the world's first completely automatic plane. Now just sit back and relax because nothing can possibly go wrong . . . go wrong . . . go wrong . . . go wrong . . ."

☆ ☆ ☆

That airplane flight was so rough that the stewardess poured the food directly into the sick sacks!

☆ ☆ ☆

Pilot: "Control tower, what time is it?"
Control tower: "What airline is this?"
Pilot: "What difference does that make?"
Control tower: "If it is United Airlines, it is 6:00 p.m.; if it is TWA, it is 1800 hours; if it is Ozark, the big hand is on the . . . "

☆ ☆ ☆

Passenger: "Say, stewardess, this is the worst steak I ever had. Don't you stewardesses even know how to serve a steak? Bring me another steak right now!"
Stewardess: "Will that be to take out?"

☆ ☆ ☆

Stewardess: "I am sorry, Mr. Jones, but we left your wife behind in Chicago."

Man: "Thank goodness! I thought I was going deaf!"

☆　☆　☆

Pilot: "Pilot to tower . . . pilot to tower . . . I am 300 miles from land . . . 600 feet high and running out of gas . . . please instruct . . . over."

Tower: "Tower to pilot . . . tower to pilot . . . repeat after me . . . Our Father, which art in heaven . . . "

☆　☆　☆

The other day one of those jumbo jets took off from New York with four hundred passengers and then had to make a forced landing in Newark because of a hernia.

☆　☆　☆

Last week I was flying on a plane and almost had a heart attack when I noticed a sign on the door of the pilot's cabin that said, "Student Pilot."

☆　☆　☆

ARMY AND POLICE

First Rookie: "I feel like punching that top sarge in the nose again!"

Second Rookie: "What do you mean, again?"

First Rookie: "I felt like it yesterday, too."

☆　☆　☆

Officer: "Soldier, do you have change for a dollar?"

Soldier: "Sure, buddy."

Officer: "That's no way to address an officer. Now, let's try that again. Soldier, do you have change for a dollar?"

Soldier: "No, sir!"

☆　☆　☆

Dad: "When I was in the Army, Harvey, we had a drill sergeant who was so tough he used to wear a wig."

Son: "What's so tough about that?"

Dad: "He used to keep it on with a nail."

☆　☆　☆

The story is told of a corporal who reported to a new regiment with a letter from his old captain, saying, "This man is a great soldier, and he'll be even better if you can cure him of his constant gambling." The new C. O. looked at him sternly and said, "I hear you're an inveterate gambler. I don't approve. It's bad for discipline. What kind of thing do you bet on?" "Practically anything, sir," said the corporal. "If you'd like, I'll bet you my next month's pay that you've got a strawberry birthmark under your right arm." The C. O. snapped, "Put down your money." He then stripped to the waist, proved conclusively he had no birthmark, and pocketed the bills on the table. He couldn't wait to phone the captain and exult, "That corporal of yours won't be in a hurry to make a bet after what I just did to him." "Don't be too sure," said the captain mournfully. "He just wagered me twenty to two hundred he'd get you to take your shirt off five minutes after he reported."

☆　☆　☆

An Army base staff that was planning war games did not want to use live ammunition. Instead they informed the men: "In place of a rifle, you go, 'Bang, bang.' In place of a knife, you go, 'Stab, stab.' In place of a hand grenade, you go, 'Lob, lob.' "

The game was in progress when one of the soldiers saw one of the enemy. He went, "Bang, bang," but nothing happened. He ran forward and went, "Stab, stab," but nothing happened. He ran back and went, "Lob, lob," but nothing happened. Finally he walked up to the enemy and said, "You are not playing fair. I went, 'Bang, bang,' and, 'Stab, stab,' and, 'Lob, lob,' and you haven't fallen dead yet!"

The enemy responded, "Rumble, rumble. I'm a tank."

☆   ☆   ☆

A very new soldier was on sentry duty at the main gate of a military outpost. His orders were clear: No car was to enter unless it had a special sticker on the windshield. A big Army car came up with a general seated in the back. The sentry said, "Halt, who goes there?" The chauffeur, a corporal, said, "General Wheeler." "I'm sorry, I can't let you through. You've got to have a sticker on the windshield." The general said, "Drive on." The sentry said, "Hold it. You really can't come through. I have orders to shoot if you try driving in without a sticker." The general repeated, "I'm telling you, son, drive on." The sentry walked up to the rear window and said, "General, I'm new at this: do I shoot you or the driver?"

☆   ☆   ☆

A blowhard Air Force major was promoted to colonel and received a brand new office. His first morning behind the desk, an airman knocked on the door and asked to speak to him. The colonel, feeling

7

the urge to impress the young airman, picked up his phone and said:

"Yes, General, thank you. Yes, I will pass that along to the President this afternoon. Yes, good-bye, sir."

Then, turning to the airman he barked, "And what do you want?"

"Nothing important, sir," said the airman. "I just came to install your telephone."

☆　☆　☆

Voice: "Hello. We need twelve vehicles in the parade square immediately. Two of them must be limousines."

Reply: "What are the limousines for? To haul those fat-slob generals around in, I bet."

Voice: "Soldier, do you know who this is speaking?"

Reply: "No, I don't."

Voice: "This is General Watson."

Reply: "Do you know who this is speaking, sir?"

Voice: "No, I don't."

Reply: "See ya 'round, fatso!"

☆　☆　☆

"Simply read the letters on that chart," ordered the draft board doctor.

"I don't see any chart," answered the draftee happily.

"You're absolutely right," snapped the doctor. "There isn't any chart. You're 1-A."

☆　☆　☆

Just before a drafted farm boy made his first parachute jump, his sergeant reminded him, "Count ten and pull the first rip cord. If it snarls, pull the second rip cord for the auxiliary chute. After you land, our truck will pick you up."

The paratrooper took a deep breath and jumped. He counted to ten, and pulled the first cord. Nothing happened. He pulled the second cord. Again, nothing happened. As he careened crazily earthward, he said to himself: "Now I'll bet that truck won't be there either!"

☆　☆　☆

A draftee went in for his physical wearing a truss and with papers that were stamped "M. E." for Medically Exempt.

Afterward a friend borrowed the truss to wear for his physical.

At the end of the examination the doctor stamped M. E. on his papers. "Does that mean I'm Medically Exempt?" he asked the doctor.

"No," replied the doctor. "M. E. stands for Middle East. Anyone who can wear a truss upside down can ride a camel."

☆　☆　☆

One day a sergeant came into the barracks and asked his men if any of them knew shorthand. The recruits thought that it would be easy duty and raised their hands.

"Good," said the sergeant. "They're shorthanded in the mess hall!"

☆　☆　☆

He: "My wife just got a ticket for speeding."

Him: "That's nothing! My wife is so bad the police gave her a season ticket."

☆　☆　☆

Woman: "Oh, Mr. Policeman! Mr. Policeman! A man is following me and I think he is crazy!"

Policeman: "I agree!"

☆　☆　☆

Policeman: "Here is your parking ticket."

Woman: "And just what do you do when you catch a real criminal?"

Policeman: "I don't know . . . all I ever catch are the innocent ones."

☆　☆　☆

A driver tucked this note under the windshield wiper of his automobile: "I've circled the block for twenty minutes. I'm late for an appointment and if I don't park here I'll lose my job. 'Forgive us our trespasses.' "

When he came back he found a parking ticket and this note: "I've circled the block for twenty years and if I don't give you a ticket, I'll lose my job. 'Lead us not into temptation.' "

☆　☆　☆

The stalled car sat dead still at a traffic light as the lights went to red, to green, to yellow, to red, to green, to yellow, to red. Finally a cop came up and said, "Pardon me, sir, but don't we have any color you like?"

☆　☆　☆

"Hello, police department? I've lost my cat and . . ."

"Sorry, sir, that's not a job for the police, we're too busy . . ."

"But you don't understand . . . this is a very intelligent cat. He's almost human. He can practically talk."

"Well, you'd better hang up, sir. He may be trying to phone you right now."

☆ ☆ ☆

"What am I supposed to do with this?" grumbled the motorist as the police clerk handed him a receipt for his traffic fine.

"Keep it," the clerk advised. "When you get four of them, you get a bicycle."

☆ ☆ ☆

Things are so bad in our town that the police department now has an unlisted telephone number.

☆ ☆ ☆

Despite what Ralph Nader says, the best safety device is a rear-view mirror with a cop in it.

☆ ☆ ☆

When the traffic cop asked the prostrate man if he got the number of the hit-and-run driver, he said, "No, but I'd recognize my wife's laugh anywhere."

☆ ☆ ☆

A policeman stopped a man driving the wrong way on a one-way street. "Didn't you see the arrow?" he demanded.

"Arrow? Honest, Officer, I didn't even see the Indians."

☆ ☆ ☆

Officer to man pacing sidewalk at 3 A.M.: "What are you doing here?"

Gentleman: "I forgot my key, Officer, and I'm waiting for my children to come home and let me in."

☆　☆　☆

A rookie officer was asked the following question on his examination paper: "How would you go about dispersing a crowd?"

He answered: "Take up an offering. That does it every time."

☆　☆　☆

Game Warden: "Fishing?"

Man without license: "No; drowning worms."

☆　☆　☆

Stranger: "Catch any fish?"

Fisherman: "Did I! I took thirty out of this stream this morning."

Stranger: "Do you know who I am? I'm the game warden."

Fisherman: "Do you know who I am? I'm the biggest liar in the country."

☆　☆　☆

Judge: "Order in this court! I'll have order in this court!"

Man: "I'll have a hamburger with onions!"

☆　☆　☆

In the traffic court of a large midwestern city, a young lady was brought before the judge to answer a ticket given her for driving through a red light. She

12

explained to his honor that she was a school teacher and requested an immediate disposal of her case in order that she might hasten on to her classes. A wild gleam came into the judge's eye. "You're a school teacher, eh?" said he. "Madam, I shall realize my lifelong ambition. I've waited years to have a school teacher in this court. Sit down at that table and write 'I went through a red light' five hundred times!"

☆　☆　☆

Several women appeared in court, each accusing the other of the trouble in the flat where they lived. The judge, with Solomon-like wisdom, called for orderly testimony. "I'll hear the oldest first," he decreed. The case closed for lack of evidence.

☆　☆　☆

Burglar: "The police are coming! Quick, jump out the window!"
Accomplice: "But we're on the thirteenth floor!"
Burglar: "This is no time to be superstitious."

☆　☆　☆

The other day a guy pointed a gun at me and said, "Stick 'em up and congratulations!" I said, "What's the congratulations for?" He said, "You are now entering a lower tax bracket."

☆　☆　☆

There's so much crime in my neighborhood the intersection lights say, "Shoot," and, "Don't shoot."

☆　☆　☆

A bank robber held up a bank. "Give me all your money."

"Here, take the books, too. I'm short ten thousand dollars."

☆   ☆   ☆

Sheriff: "Excuse me for being nervous," he apologized as he slipped the noose over the condemned man's head. "This is my first hanging."
Man: "Mine too!"

☆   ☆   ☆

A fellow walked up to me and said, "Stick 'em down."
I said, "You mean stick 'em up."
He said, "No wonder I haven't made any money."

☆   ☆   ☆

The story is told of a young Czechoslovakian, a Russian officer, a little old lady, and an attractive young woman riding on a train.
Shortly after the train entered a dark tunnel, the passengers heard a kiss, then a loud slap.
The girl thought: "Isn't that odd the Russian tried to kiss the old lady and not me?"
The old lady thought: "That is a good girl with fine morals."
The Russian officer thought: "That Czech is a smart fellow; he steals a kiss and I get slapped."
The Czech thought: "Perfect. I kiss the back of my hand, clout a Russian officer, and get away with it."

☆   ☆   ☆

A burglar entered the house of a Quaker and proceeded to rob it. The Quaker heard noises and took his shotgun downstairs and found the burglar. He aimed his gun and said gently: "Friend, I mean thee no harm, but thou standest where I am about to shoot."

☆   ☆   ☆

Said the FBI agent to the bank teller after the bank was robbed for the third time by the same bandit: "Did you notice anything special about the man?"

"Yes, he seemed better dressed each time."

☆   ☆   ☆

ATHEISTS

They have all sorts of new services today. Now they've got a dial-a-prayer service for atheists. You call a number and nobody answers.

☆   ☆   ☆

Sign on the tomb of an atheist:
HERE LIES AN ATHEIST ALL DRESSED UP
AND NO PLACE TO GO.

☆   ☆   ☆

An atheist is a man who has no invisible means of support.

☆   ☆   ☆

Pity the poor atheist who feels grateful but has no one to thank.

☆   ☆   ☆

15

Atheists are really on the spot; they have to sing "Hmmmmmm bless America."

☆　☆　☆

Three atheists were trying to bother a young Baptist minister.

"I think I will move to Nevada," said the first atheist, "only 25 percent of the people are Baptists."

"No, I think I would rather live in Colorado," said the second man; "only 10 percent of the people are Baptists."

"Better yet," said the third atheist, "is New Mexico . . . only 5 percent there are Baptists."

"I think the best place for you all is Hades," said the minister. "There are no Baptists there!"

☆　☆　☆

I once wanted to become an atheist but I gave up the idea. They have no holidays.

☆　☆　☆

An atheist was teasing Bill about his religious beliefs. "Come on now, Bill," he said, "do you really believe that when you die you'll go up to heaven and fly around with wings? I understand it's not warm up there like where I'm going when I die. How in the world are you going to get your coat on over those wings?"

Bill replied, "The same way you are going to get your trousers over your tail!"

☆　☆　☆

Overheard: "I'm an atheist, thank God."

☆　☆　☆

Did you hear about the son of the atheists who asked his parents: "Do you think God knows we don't believe in him?"

☆　☆　☆

BALD

If a man is bald in front, he's a thinker. If he's bald in the back, he is a lover. If he's bald in front and back, he thinks he's a lover.

☆　☆　☆

"Papa, are you growing taller all the time?"
"No, my child. Why do you ask?"
" 'Cause the top of your head is poking up through your hair."

☆　☆　☆

A bald man's retort:. "In the beginning God created all men bald; later he became ashamed of some and covered them up with hair."

☆　☆　☆

He has wavy hair . . . it's waving goodbye.

☆　☆　☆

He's not baldheaded . . . he just has flesh-colored hair.

☆　☆　☆

He's a man of polish . . . mostly around his head.

There's one proverb that really depresses him: "Hair today, gone tomorrow."

☆　☆　☆

He has less hair to comb, but more face to wash.

☆　☆　☆

It's not that he's baldheaded . . . he just has a tall face.

☆　☆　☆

There's one thing about baldness . . . it's neat.

☆　☆　☆

There's a new remedy on the market for baldness. It's made of alum and persimmon juice. It doesn't grow hair, but it shrinks your head to fit what hair you have.

☆　☆　☆

He's so bald he walks into a barber shop and asks for a shave and a shave.

☆　☆　☆

He is so bald that it looks like his neck is blowing a bubble.

☆　☆　☆

BARBERS

A man entered a barber shop and asked for a shave. After the shave, the barber said, "That will be 10 cents, please."

"But," said the man, "your sign says $1.25 for a shave. How come only 10 cents?"

The barber answered, "Once in awhile we get a guy that is all mouth and we only charge him a dime!"

☆   ☆   ☆

I couldn't stand my boy's long hair any longer, so I dragged him with me and ordered, "Give him a crew cut." The barber did just that, and so help me, I found I'd been bringing up somebody else's son!

☆   ☆   ☆

Did you hear about the rock and roll singer who wore a hearing aid for three years . . . then found out he only needed a haircut.

☆   ☆   ☆

I've got a sixteen-year-old son who was 6'3" until he got a haircut. Now he is 5'8".

☆   ☆   ☆

The customer settled himself and let the barber put the towel around him. Then he told the barber, "Before we start, I know the weather's awful. I don't care who wins the next big fight, and I don't bet on the horse races. I know I'm getting thin on top, but I don't mind. Now get on with it."

"Well, sir, if you don't mind," said the barber, "I'll

be able to concentrate better if you don't talk so much!"

☆ ☆ ☆

A man entered a barber shop and said: "I am tired of looking like everyone else! I want a change! Part my hair from ear to ear!"

"Are you sure?"

"Yes!" said the man.

The barber did as he was told and a satisfied customer left the shop.

Three hours passed and the man re-entered the shop. "Put it back the way it was," he said.

"What's the matter?" said the barber. "Are you tired of being a nonconformist already?"

"No," he replied, "I'm tired of people whispering in my nose!"

☆ ☆ ☆

A cute girl was giving a manicure to a man in the barber shop.

The man said, "How about a date later?"

She said, "I'm married."

"So call up your husband and tell him you're going to visit a girl friend."

She said, "You tell him yourself . . . he's shaving you."

☆ ☆ ☆

Customer: (twice nicked by the barber's razor) "Hey, barber, gimme a glass of water."

Barber: "What's wrong, sir? Hair in your mouth?"

Customer: "No, I want to see if my neck leaks."

☆ ☆ ☆

BIBLE QUIZ

Q: "When were automobiles first mentioned in the Bible?"
A: "When Elijah went up on high."

☆　　☆　　☆

Q: "What simple affliction brought about the death of Samson?"
A: "Fallen arches."

☆　　☆　　☆

Q: "Who was the most successful physician in the Bible?"
A: "Job; he had the most patience (patients)."

☆　　☆　　☆

Q: "Who was the best financier in the Bible?"
A: "Noah; he floated his stock while the whole world was in liquidation."

☆　　☆　　☆

Q: "Who was the straightest man in the Bible?"
A: "Joseph. Pharaoh made a ruler out of him."

☆　　☆　　☆

Q: "Where is tennis mentioned in the Bible?"
A: "When Joseph served in Pharaoh's court."

☆　　☆　　☆

Q: "What animal took the most baggage into the ark?"

A: "The elephant. He took his trunk, while the fox and the rooster only took a brush and comb."

☆ ☆ ☆

Q: "What man in the Bible had no parents?"
A: "Joshua, the son of Nun."

☆ ☆ ☆

Q: "Who is the smallest man in the Bible?"
A: "Some people believe that it was Zacchaeus. Others believe it was Nehemiah (Ne-high-a-miah), or Bildad, the Shuhite. But in reality it was Peter, the disciple—he slept on his watch!"

☆ ☆ ☆

Q: "When was baseball mentioned in the Bible?"
A: "When Rebecca walked to the well with the pitcher, and when the Prodigal Son made a home run."

☆ ☆ ☆

Q: "Who is the first man mentioned in the Bible?"
A: "Chap I."

☆ ☆ ☆

Q: "When was money first mentioned in the Bible?"
A: "When the dove brought the green back to the ark."

☆ ☆ ☆

Q: Who was the most popular actor in the Bible?"
A: "Samson. He brought the house down."

☆ ☆ ☆

Q: "Do you know how you can tell that David was older than Goliath?"

A: "Because David rocked Goliath to sleep!"

☆   ☆   ☆

Ned: "What instructions did Noah give his sons about fishing off the ark?"

Fred: "I don't know."

Ned: "Go easy on the bait, boys. I only have two worms."

☆   ☆   ☆

Joe: "Was there any money on Noah's ark?"

Moe: "Yes. The duck took a bill, the frog took a green back, and the skunk took a scent."

☆   ☆   ☆

Q: "Why didn't they play cards on Noah's ark?"

A: "Because Noah sat on the deck."

☆   ☆   ☆

Q: "How did Jonah feel when the great fish swallowed him?"

A: "Down in the mouth."

☆   ☆   ☆

Q: "When is high financing first mentioned in the Bible?"

A: "When Pharaoh's daughter took a little prophet (profit) from the bulrushes."

☆   ☆   ☆

Q: "When did Moses sleep with five people in one bed?"

A: "When he slept with his forefathers."

☆　　☆　　☆

Teacher: "Where was Solomon's temple?"
Student: "On the side of his head."

☆　　☆　　☆

Fay: "How long a period of time did Cain hate his brother?"
Ray: "As long as he was Abel."

☆　　☆　　☆

BOY AND GIRL

"When I went out with Fred, I had to slap his face five times."
"Was he that fresh?"
"No! I thought he was dead!"

☆　　☆　　☆

Girl: "Did you kiss me when the lights were out?"
Boy: "No!"
Girl: "It must have been that fellow over there!"
Boy, starting to get up: "I'll teach him a thing or two!"
Girl: "You couldn't teach him a thing!"

☆　　☆　　☆

"Well, and how are you getting on with your courtship of the banker's daughter?"
"Not so bad. I'm getting some encouragement now."

"Really, is she beginning to smile sweetly on you or something?"

"Not exactly, but last night she told me she had said 'no' for the last time."

☆ ☆ ☆

Girl: "The man I marry must be brave as a lion, but not forward; handsome as Apollo, but not conceited; wise as Solomon, but meek as a lamb; a man who is kind to every woman, but loves only me."

Boy: "How lucky we met!"

☆ ☆ ☆

"Without you, everything is dark and dreary . . . the clouds gather and the wind beats the rain . . . then comes the warm sun . . . you are like a rainbow."

"Is this a proposal or a weather report?"

☆ ☆ ☆

Joe: "What's so unusual about your girlfriend?"
Moe: "She chews on her nails."
Joe: "Lots of girls chew on their nails."
Moe: "Toenails?"

☆ ☆ ☆

"Why does my sweetheart always close her eyes when I kiss her?"

"Look in the mirror, and you'll know."

☆ ☆ ☆

John: "You must marry me . . . I love you, there can be no other . . . "

Mary: "But, John, I don't love you . . . you must find some other woman . . . some beautiful woman . . . "

John: "But I don't want a beautiful woman . . . I want you."

☆ ☆ ☆

Jill: "What fruit lasted the longest in Noah's ark?"
Bill: "I don't know."
Jill: "The preserved pairs."

☆ ☆ ☆

Boy: "You know, sweetheart, since I met you, I can't eat . . . I can't sleep . . . I can't drink . . . "
Girl: "Why not?"
Boy: "I'm broke!"

☆ ☆ ☆

"My girlfriend takes advantage of me."
"What do you mean?"
"I invited her out to dinner and she asked me if she could bring a date!"

☆ ☆ ☆

After a blind date a fellow mentioned to his friend: "After I got home last night, I felt a lump in my throat." "You really like her, huh?" "No, she's a karate expert."

☆ ☆ ☆

Boy: "Will you marry me?"
Girl: "No, but I'll always admire your good taste."

☆ ☆ ☆

"Do you have the book *Man, Master of Women?*" a young man asked the lady librarian.

"Fiction counter to your left," the librarian replied.

☆　☆　☆

Boy, with one hand cupped over the other: "If you can guess what I have in my hand, I'll take you out tonight."

Girl: "An elephant!"

Boy: "Nope! But that's close enough. I'll pick you up at 7:30."

☆　☆　☆

A school boy took home a library book whose cover read *How to Hug*, only to discover that it was Volume VII of an encyclopedia!

☆　☆　☆

Boy: "Ah, look at the cow and the calf rubbing noses in the pasture. That sight makes me want to do the same."

Girl: "Well, go ahead . . . it's your cow."

☆　☆　☆

Girl: "Do you think you could be happy with a girl like me?"

Boy: "Perhaps, if she isn't too much like you."

☆　☆　☆

"How come you go steady with Eloise?"
"She's different from other girls."
"How so?"
"She's the only girl who will go with me."

☆　☆　☆

27

He: "Oh, my dear, how can I leave you?"
She: "By train, plane, or taxi!"

☆　　☆　　☆

Boy: "Gladys, do you love me?"
Girl: "Yeah."
Boy: "Would you be willing to live on my income?"
Girl: "Yes, if you'll get another for yourself."

☆　　☆　　☆

Boy: "Darling, I've lost all my money. I haven't a cent in the world."
Girl: "That won't make any difference, dear. I'll love you just as much ... even if I never see you again.

☆　　☆　　☆

Girl: "I'm telling you for the last time; you can't kiss me!"
Boy: "Oh, I knew you would weaken."

☆　　☆　　☆

Girl: "Do you love me?"
Boy: "Yes, dear."
Girl: "Would you die for me?"
Boy: "No ... mine is an undying love."

☆　　☆　　☆

John: "Don't you think I'm rather good looking?"
Judy: "In a way."
John: "What kind of way?"
Judy: "Away off."

☆　　☆　　☆

Bill: "That girl in the red dress isn't very smart."
Phil: "I know. She hasn't paid any attention to me either."

☆　☆　☆

Boy: "What would I have to give you for one little kiss?"
Girl: "Chloroform!"

☆　☆　☆

Harry: "My girlfriend has a huge lower lip, but I don't mind."
Gary: "You don't?"
Harry: "No, her upper lip covers it!"

☆　☆　☆

She: "Look at my engagement ring."
Chi-Chi: "That's a lovely ring. It's nice to know you're not marrying a spendthrift."

☆　☆　☆

Boy: "Boy, if I had a nickel for every girl I'd kissed . . ."
Girl: "You'd be able to buy a pack of gum!"

☆　☆　☆

CANNIBALS

My uncle is a cannibal. He's been living on us for twenty years!

☆　☆　☆

First Cannibal: "We've just captured a movie star."
Second Cannibal: "Great! I was hoping for a good ham sandwich."

☆ ☆ ☆

It was a lucky day in the cannibal village. They had an explorer in the pot, and about to be cooked. The chief asked the victim if he had any last words to say. The explorer gasped, "Yes. I'm smoking more now and enjoying it less."

☆ ☆ ☆

Then there's the missionary the cannibal couldn't boil. He was a friar.

☆ ☆ ☆

Cannibal Cook: "Shall I stew both of these Navy cooks?"
Cannibal King: "No. One's enough. Too many cooks spoil the broth."

☆ ☆ ☆

A resourceful missionary fell into the hands of a band of cannibals. "Going to eat me, I take it," said the missionary. "You wouldn't like me." He took out his pocketknife, sliced a piece from the calf of his leg, and handed it to the chief. "Try it and see for yourself," he urged. The chief took one bite, grunted and spat.

The missionary remained on the island fifty years. He had a cork leg.

☆ ☆ ☆

CHURCH, PREACHERS, AND SUNDAY SCHOOL

Reverend Henry Ward Beecher entered Plymouth Church one Sunday and found several letters awaiting him. He opened one and found it contained the single word, "Fool." Quietly and with becoming seriousness he announced to the congregation the fact in these words:

"I have known many an instance of a man writing a letter and forgetting to sign his name, but this is the only instance I have ever known of a man signing his name and forgetting to write the letter."

☆ ☆ ☆

So this big-wheel Russian is riding along when he sees a peasant, kneeling in the middle of a field, praying. He stops the car, stomps over and says:

"Aha! You waste your time like this instead of plowing and planting for the Party!"

"But, Commissar, I'm praying for the Party!"

"Praying for the Party! Huh! And years ago, you probably prayed for the Czar!"

"I did, Commissar."

"Well . . . look what happened to him!"

"Right!"

☆ ☆ ☆

Did you hear about the country parson who decided to buy himself a horse? The dealer assured him that the one he selected was a perfect choice. "This here horse," he said, "has lived all his life in a religious atmosphere. So remember that he'll never start if you order 'Giddyap.' You've got to say, 'Praise the Lord.' Likewise, a 'Whoa' will never make him stop. You've got to say, 'Amen.'

Thus forewarned, the parson paid for the horse, mounted him, and with a cheery "Praise the Lord" sent him cantering off in the direction of the parson's parish. Suddenly, however, he noticed that the road ahead had been washed out, leaving a chasm two hundred yards deep. In a panic, he forgot his instructions and cried "Whoa" in vain several times. The horse just cantered on. At the very last moment he remembered to cry "Amen" ... and the horse stopped short at the very brink of the chasm. But alas! That's when the parson, out of force of habit, murmured fervently, "Praise the Lord!"

☆　☆　☆

Wife: "Did you see that hat Mrs. Jones wore to church?"

Husband: "No!"

Wife: "Did you see the new dress Mrs. Smith had on?"

Husband: "No!"

Wife: "A lot of good it does you to go to church!"

☆　☆　☆

A conscientious minister decided to get acquainted with a new family in his congregation and called on them one spring evening. After his knock on the door, a lilting voice from within called out, "Is that you, Angel?" "No," replied the minister, "but I'm from the same department."

☆　☆　☆

A young businessman returned home after a tough day at the office and found his two daughters, both of about kindergarten age, acting up pretty boisterously. He gave them a moderately severe scolding and sent them off to bed. The next morning he found a note stuck on his bedroom door: "Be good to your children and they will be good to you. God."

☆ ☆ ☆

We've been letting our six-year-old go to sleep listening to the radio, and I'm beginning to wonder if it's a good idea. Last night he said his prayers and wound up with: "And God bless Mommy and Daddy and Sister. Amen . . . and FM!"

☆ ☆ ☆

Did you hear the one about the ministers who formed a bowling team? Called themselves the Holy Rollers.

☆ ☆ ☆

A preacher was called upon to substitute for the regular minister, who had failed to reach the church because he was delayed in a snowstorm. The speaker began by explaining the meaning of a substitute. "If you break a window," he said, "and then place a cardboard there instead, that is a substitute."

After the sermon, a woman who had listened intently shook hands with him, and wishing to compliment him, said, "You were no substitute . . . you were a real pane!"

☆ ☆ ☆

The sermon went on and on and on in the heat of the church. At last the minister paused and asked, "What more, my friends, can I say?"

In the back of the church a voice offered earnestly: "Amen!"

☆ ☆ ☆

The popular preacher, Charles Spurgeon, was admonishing a class of divinity students on the importance of making the facial expressions harmonize with the speech in delivering sermons. "When you speak of heaven," he said, "let your face light up and be irradiated with a heavenly gleam. Let your eyes shine with reflected glory. And when you speak of hell . . . well, then your everyday face will do."

☆　　☆　　☆

One pastor said that his church people would be the first to go up in the rapture. He gave his reason: "The Bible says: 'The dead in Christ shall rise first.' "

☆　　☆　　☆

Little William was saying his prayers one night. His mother tiptoed up and heard him say, "And please make Tommy stop throwing things at me. You may remember, I've mentioned this before. He's still doing it."

☆　　☆　　☆

The Sunday school teacher was describing how Lot's wife looked back and suddenly turned into a pillar of salt.

"My mother looked back once while she was driving," contributed little Johnny, "and she turned into a telephone pole."

☆　　☆　　☆

Little Jane, whose grandmother was visiting her family, was going to bed when her mother called:

"Don't forget, dear, to include Grandma in your prayers tonight, that God should bless her and let her live to be very, very old."

"Oh, she's old enough,", replied Jane. "I'd rather pray that God would make her young."

☆ ☆ ☆

A young woman named Murphy was teaching a Sunday school class the 23rd Psalm. As the little voices chorused out, she seemed somewhere to detect a false note. She heard the children one by one, until at last she came across one little boy who was concluding the psalm with the words, "Surely good Miss Murphy shall follow me all the days of my life."

☆ ☆ ☆

A young girl went to her pastor and confessed that she feared she had incurred the sin of vanity. "What makes you think that?" asked the minister. "Because every morning when I look into the mirror I think how beautiful I am."

"Never fear, my girl," was the reassuring reply. "That isn't a sin, it's only a mistake."

☆ ☆ ☆

A very foul-mouthed man met the local pastor on the street one day and said, "Now, where in hell have I seen you?" To which the pastor replied, "From where in hell do you come, sir?"

☆ ☆ ☆

A minister wound up the services one morning by saying, "Next Sunday I am going to preach on the subject of liars. And in this connection, as a preparation for my discourse, I should like you all to read the 17th chapter of Mark." On the following Sunday, the preacher rose to begin, and said, "Now, then, all of you who have done as I requested and read the

17th chapter of Mark, please raise your hands."
Nearly every hand in the congregation went up. Then
said the preacher, "You are the people I want to talk
to. There is no 17th chapter of Mark!"

☆　　☆　　☆

"I never go to church," boasted a wandering member. "Perhaps you have noticed that?"

"Yes, I have noticed that," said his pastor.

"Well, the reason I don't go is that there are so many hypocrites there."

"Oh, don't let that keep you away," replied the pastor, smiling blandly. "There is always room for one more, you know."

☆　　☆　　☆

Q: Why are there so few men with whiskers in heaven?

A: Because most men get in by a close shave.

☆　　☆　　☆

Two men fishing on Sunday morning were feeling pretty guilty, especially since the fish didn't bite. One said to the other, "I guess I should have stayed home and gone to church."

To which the other angler replied lazily; "I couldn't have gone to church, anyway . . . my wife's sick in bed."

☆　　☆　　☆

Little Susie, a six-year-old, complained, "Mother, I've got a stomach-ache."

"That's because your stomach is empty," the mother replied. "You would feel better if you had something in it."

That afternoon the minister called, and in conversation remarked he had been suffering all day with a severe headache.

Susie perked up. "That's because it's empty," she said. "You'd feel better if you had something in it."

☆　☆　☆

A Baptist minister rushed down to the train station every single day to watch the Sunset Limited go by. There was no chore he wouldn't interrupt to carry out his ritual. Members of his congregation deemed his eccentricity juvenile and frivolous, and asked him to give it up. "No, gentlemen," he said firmly. "I preach your sermons, teach your Sunday school, bury your dead, marry you, run your charities, chairman every drive it pleases you to conduct. I won't give up seeing that Southern Pacific train every day. I love it! It's the only thing in this town I don't have to push!"

☆　☆　☆

"Why do you keep reading your Bible all day long?" a youngster demanded of his aged grandfather. "Well," he explained, "you might say I was cramming for my final examinations."

☆　☆　☆

A dignified old clergyman owned a parrot of whom he was exceedingly fond, but the bird had picked up an appalling vocabulary of cuss words from a previous owner and, after a series of embarrassing episodes, the clergyman decided he would have to kill his pet. A lady in his parish suggested a last-ditch remedy. "I have a female parrot," she said, "who is an absolute saint. She sits quietly on her perch and says nothing but, 'Let's pray.' Why don't you bring your parrot over and see if my own bird's good influence doesn't reform him?"

37

The clergyman said it was worth a trial, and the next night he arrived with his pet tucked under his arm. The bird took one look at the lady parrot and chirped, "Hi, toots. How about a little kiss?" "My prayers have been answered," said the lady parrot gleefully.

☆　　☆　　☆

A minister spoke to a deacon and said, "I'm told you went to the ball game instead of church this morning." "That's a lie," said the deacon, "and here's the fish to prove it."

☆　　☆　　☆

Today more and more hippies are looking to religion for the answer to their problems. Last Sunday, a hippie went to church and he was so overwhelmed by the sermon he grabbed the preacher's hand when he left the church and said, "Dad, I read you; that sermon was the most; it was gone; you were right on." The preacher said, "I'm afraid I don't understand." The hippie said, "Yes, you do, dad. In fact, I liked it so gone, I put twenty samolas in the collection plate." The preacher said, "Oh, crazy, man, crazy!"

☆　　☆　　☆

A hat was passed around a church congregation for taking up an offering for the visiting minister.

Presently it was returned to him . . . conspicuously and embarrassingly empty. Slowly and deliberately, the parson inverted the hat and shook it meaningfully. Then raising his eyes to heaven, he exclaimed fervently, "I thank thee, dear Lord, that I got my hat back from this congregation."

☆　　☆　　☆

Hoping to develop his son's character, a father once gave him a penny and a quarter as he was leaving for Sunday school. "Now, Bill, you put whichever one you want in the offering plate," he said.

When the boy returned, his father asked which coin he had given. Bill answered, "Well, just before they sent around the plate the preacher said, 'The Lord loveth a cheerful giver,' and I knew I could give the penny a lot more cheerfully than I could give the quarter, so I gave it."

☆　☆　☆

A minister asked a little girl what she thought of her first church service.

"The music was nice," she said, "but the commercial was too long."

☆　☆　☆

Sammy: "You know what it means when a preacher steps into the pulpit, removes his watch and places it on the pulpit?"

Danny: "Yeah, nothing!"

☆　☆　☆

A couple was touring the Capitol in Washington and the guide pointed to a tall, benevolent gentleman as the congressional chaplain.

The lady asked, "What does the chaplain do? Does he pray for the Senate or House?"

The guide answered, "No, he gets up, looks at the congress, then prays for the country!"

☆　☆　☆

During a business meeting in a small mountain church, one of the deacons said, "Pastor, I think we need a chandelier for the church."

39

"No," replied another deacon. "I'm against it."

"Why don't you think we need a chandelier, brother deacon?" asked the pastor.

"Well, first, nobody in the church can spell it; second, nobody in the church can play it; and, third, what this church needs, above all else, is mo' light!"

☆　☆　☆

The three sons of a lawyer, a doctor, and a minister, respectively, were talking about how much money their fathers made.

The lawyer's son said, "My father goes into court on a case and often comes home with as much as fifteen hundred dollars."

The doctor's son said, "My father performs an operation and earns as much as two thousand dollars for it."

The minister's son, determined not to be outdone, said, "That's nothing. My father preaches for just twenty minutes on Sunday morning and it takes four men to carry the money."

☆　☆　☆

The new preacher, at his first service, had a pitcher of water and a glass on the pulpit. As he preached, he drank until the pitcher of water was completely gone.

After the service someone asked an old woman of the church, "How did you like the new pastor?"

"Fine," she said, "but he's the first windmill I ever saw that was run by water."

☆　☆　☆

A minister married a couple. The woman had on a veil and he could not see her face. After the ceremony, the man asked the minister, "How much do I owe you?"

"No charge," replied the minister.

"But I want to show my appreciation." So the man gave him fifty cents.

About that time the bride pulled off her veil, and the minister, looking at the bride, gave the man twenty-five cents change.

☆   ☆   ☆

After a long, dry sermon, the minister announced that he wished to meet with the church board following the close of the service. The first man to arrive was a stranger. "You misunderstood my announcement. This is a meeting of the board," said the minister.

"I know," said the man, "but if there is anyone here more bored than I am, I'd like to meet him."

☆   ☆   ☆

There was a certain energetic young preacher who had a thriving country church. He was always prodding his people to do greater things for God. He spent much time in preparation of his sermons. There was a deacon in his congregation who did little and seemed to care less. It caused the young preacher much concern. On several occasions the preacher would tell him exactly what he thought. The old deacon never caught the point. The old deacon always thought he was referring to someone else. One Sunday, the preacher made it plainer as to whom he was talking. Following the service the deacon said, "Preacher, you sure told them today."

The next sermon was still more pointed than ever. Again the deacon said, "Preacher, you sure told them today."

The next Sunday it rained so hard that no one was at the church except this one deacon. The preacher thought that he would now know about whom he was talking. The sermon went straight to the deacon who was the only one in the congregation. Following the service, the deacon walked up to the preacher and said, "Preacher, you sure told them if they had been here."

☆   ☆   ☆

A Quaker became exasperated with his cow for kicking over a pail of milk.

He warned, "Thou knowest that, because of my religion, I can't punish thee. But if thee doeth that again, I will sell thee to a Baptist preacher and he will kick thee so thee won't be able to kick it over again!"

☆   ☆   ☆

A Sunday school teacher asked Little Willie who the first man in the Bible was.

"Hoss," said Willie.

"Wrong," said the teacher. "It was Adam."

"Ah, shucks!" Willie replied. "I knew it was one of those Cartwrights."

☆   ☆   ☆

My son is such an introvert he can't even lead in silent prayer.

☆   ☆   ☆

A minister forgot the name of a couple he was going to marry so he said from the pulpit, "Will those wishing to be united in holy matrimony please come forward after the service."

After the service thirteen old maids came forward.

☆   ☆   ☆

A new preacher had just begun his sermon. He was a little nervous and about ten minutes into the talk his mind went blank. He remembered what they had taught him in seminary when a situation like this would arise—repeat your last point. Often this would help you remember what is coming next. So he thought he would give it a try.

"Behold, I come quickly," he said. Still his mind was blank. He thought he would try it again. "Behold I come quickly." Still nothing.

He tried it one more time with such force he fell forward, knocking the pulpit to one side, tripping over a flower pot and falling into the lap of a little old lady in the front row.

The young preacher apologized and tried to explain what happened. "That's all right, young man," said the little old lady. "It was my fault. I should have gotten out of the way. You told me three times you were coming!"

☆　　☆　　☆

A new group of male applicants had just arrived in heaven.

Peter looked them over and ordered, "All men who were henpecked on earth, please step to the left; all those who were bosses in their own homes, step to the right."

The line quickly formed on the left. Only one man stepped to the right.

Peter looked at the frail little man standing by himself and inquired, "What makes you think you belong on that side?"

Without hesitation, the meek little man explained, "Because this is where my wife told me to stand."

☆　　☆　　☆

Old Pete was very close to dying but made a miraculous recovery. In the hospital his pastor came to visit him and the conversation went like this:

"Tell me, Pete, when you were so near death's door, did you feel afraid to meet your Maker?"

"No, Pastor," said Pete. "It was the other man I was afraid of!"

☆　☆　☆

A Sunday school teacher asked her students to draw a picture of the Holy Family. After the pictures were brought to her, she saw that some of the youngsters had drawn the conventional pictures—the Holy Family and the manger, the Holy Family riding on the mule, etc.

But she called up one little boy to ask him to explain his drawing, which showed an airplane with four heads sticking out of the plane windows.

She said, "I can understand you drew three of the heads to show Joseph, Mary and Jesus. But who's the fourth head?"

"Oh," answered the boy, "that's Pontius the pilot!"

☆　☆　☆

"You're a minister, huh?"

"Yes, I am."

"What church?"

"Baptist."

"Oh, you're the narrow-minded bunch that believes only their group is going to make it to heaven."

"I'm even more narrow minded than that. I don't think all of *our* group are going to make it!"

☆　☆　☆

Pastor: "Isn't this a beautiful church? Here is a plaque for the men who died in the service."

Man: "Which one? . . . morning or evening?"

☆　☆　☆

One friend to another, "You drive the car and I'll pray."

"What's the matter; don't you trust my driving?"

"Don't you trust my praying?"

☆ ☆ ☆

Member: "Pastor, how did you get that cut on your face?"

Pastor: "I was thinking about my sermon this morning and wasn't concentrating on what I was doing and cut myself while shaving."

Member: "That's too bad! Next time you had better concentrate on your shaving and cut your sermon!

☆ ☆ ☆

A parishioner had dozed off to sleep during the morning service.

"Will all who want to go to heaven stand?" the preacher asked.

All stood, except the sleeping parishioner.

After they sat down, the pastor continued: "Well, will all who want to go to the other place stand?"

Someone suddenly dropped a songbook and the sleeping man jumped to his feet and stood sheepishly facing the preacher. He mumbled confusedly, "Well, preacher, I don't know what we're voting for, but it looks like you and I are the only ones for it."

☆ ☆ ☆

Right in the middle of the service, and just before the sermon, one of the congregation remembered she had forgotten to turn off the gas under the roast. Hurriedly she scribbled a note and passed it to the usher to give to her husband. Unfortunately, the usher misunderstood her intention and took it to the pulpit. Unfolding the note, the preacher read aloud, "Please go home and turn off the gas."

☆ ☆ ☆

Several churches in the South decided to hold union services. The leader was a Baptist and proud of his denomination.

"How many Baptists are here?" he asked on the first night of the revival.

All except one little lady raised their hands.

"Lady, what are you?" asked the leader.

"I'm a Methodist," meekly replied the lady.

"Why are you a Methodist?" queried the leader.

"Well," replied the little old lady, "my grandparents were Methodists, my mother was a Methodist, and my late husband was a Methodist."

"Well," retorted the leader, "just supposing all your relatives had been morons, what would that have made you?"

"Oh, I see. A Baptist, I suppose," the lady replied meekly.

☆ ☆ ☆

"Some people say the Baptist denomination started with John the Baptist, but it was much earlier than that," said a great Baptist leader as he spoke to a large gathering of Baptist ministers. "In fact, it started 'way over in the Old Testament. In the 13th chapter of Genesis, it says Lot said to Abraham, 'You go your way and I'll go mine.' That's when the Baptists began."

☆ ☆ ☆

A little boy forgot his lines in a Sunday school presentation. His mother was in the front row to prompt him. She gestured and formed the words silently with her lips, but it did not help. Her son's memory was blank.

Finally she leaned forward and whispered the cue, "I am the light of the world."

The child beamed and with great feeling and a loud, clear voice said, "My mother is the light of the world."

☆　☆　☆

Clara: "My pastor is so good he can talk on any subject for an hour."

Sarah: "That's nothing! My pastor can talk for an hour without a subject!"

☆　☆　☆

Pastor: "Say, deacon, a mule died out in front of the church."

Deacon: "Well, it's the job of *you* ministers to look after the dead. Why tell me?"

Pastor: "You're right; it is my job. But we always notify the next of kin."

☆　☆　☆

Preacher: "Please take it easy on the bill for repairing my car. Remember, I am a poor preacher."

Mechanic: "I know; I heard you Sunday!"

☆　☆　☆

The grief-stricken man threw himself across the grave and cried bitterly, "My life, how senseless it is! How worthless is everything about me because you are gone. If only you hadn't died, if only fate had not been so cruel as to take you from this world, how different everything would have been."

A clergyman happened by and to soothe the man

he offered a prayer. Afterward he said, "I assume the person lying beneath this mound of earth was someone of importance to you."

"Importance? Indeed it was," moaned the man. "It's my wife's first husband!"

☆ ☆ ☆

Visitor: "Pastor, how many of your members are active?"

Pastor: "They all are! Some are active for the Lord and the rest are active for the devil!"

☆ ☆ ☆

First Pastor: "I hear you had a revival."

Second Pastor: "Yes, we did."

First Pastor: "How many additions did you have?"

Second Pastor: "We didn't have any additions but we had some blessed subtractions."

☆ ☆ ☆

Two lawyers were bosom friends. Much to the amazement of one, the other became a Sunday school teacher. "I bet you don't even know the Lord's Prayer," he fumed.

"Everybody knows that," the other replied. "It's, 'Now I lay me down to sleep . . . ' "

"You win," said the other admiringly. "I didn't know you knew so much about the Bible."

☆ ☆ ☆

The parson of a tiny congregation in Arkansas disappeared one night with the entire church treasury, and the local constable set out to capture him. This he did, dragging the culprit back by the collar a week later. "Here's the varmint, folks," announced the constable grimly. "I'm sorry to say he's already squandered our money, but I drug him back so we can make him preach it out."

☆　☆　☆

Member: "How are you feeling, pastor?"
Pastor: "Better."
Member: "We had a committee meeting the other night and they voted to send you this get-well card. The motion passed 4 to 3!"

☆　☆　☆

A Sunday school teacher asked a little girl if she said her prayers every night.
"No, not every night," declared the child. " 'Cause some nights I don't want anything!"

☆　☆　☆

The chaplain was passing through the prison garment factory. "Sewing?" he said to a prisoner who was at work. "No, chaplain," replied the prisoner gloomily; "reaping!"

☆　☆　☆

Correcting Sunday school lessons one day, a teacher found that little Jimmy had written, "Harold be thy name," as well as "Give us this day our jelly bread."

☆　☆　☆

A Sunday school teacher asked her class to draw a picture illustrating a Bible story. One paper handed in contained a picture of a big car. An old man, with long whiskers flying in the breeze, was driving. A man and a woman were seated in the back of the car.

Puzzled, the teacher asked little Johnny to explain his drawing. "Why, that is God. He is driving Adam and Eve out of the Garden of Eden."

☆　☆　☆

A hungry little boy was beginning to eat his dinner when his father reminded him that they hadn't prayed.

"We don't have to," said the little boy. "Mommy is a good cook!"

☆　☆　☆

Little Mary, the daughter of a radio announcer, was invited to a friend's house for dinner. The hostess asked if Mary would honor them by saying grace.

Delighted, the little girl cleared her throat, looked at her wrist watch and said, "This food, friends, is coming to you through the courtesy of Almighty God!"

☆　☆　☆

On the way home from church a little boy asked his mother, "Is it true, Mommy, that we are made of dust?"

"Yes, darling."

"And do we go back to dust again when we die?"

"Yes, dear."

"Well, Mommy, when I said my prayers last night and looked under the bed, I found someone who is either coming or going."

☆　☆　☆

One Sunday a farmer went to church. When he entered he saw that he and the preacher were the only ones present. The preacher asked the farmer if he wanted him to go ahead and preach. The farmer said, "I'm not too smart, but if I went to feed my cattle and only one showed up, I'd feed him." So the minister began his sermon.

One hour passed, then two hours, then two-and-a-half hours. The preacher finally finished and came down to ask the farmer how he had liked the sermon.

The farmer answered slowly, "Well, I'm not very smart, but if I went to feed my cattle and only one showed up, I sure wouldn't feed him all the hay."

☆　☆　☆

Little Susie concluded her prayer by saying: "Dear God, before I finish, please take care of Daddy, take care of Mommy, take care of my baby brother, Grandma, and Grandpa . . . and please, God, take care of yourself, or else we're all sunk!"

☆　☆　☆

A Sunday school teacher asked her class to write a composition on the story of Samson. One teen-age girl wrote, "Samson wasn't so unusual. The boys I know brag about their strength and wear their hair long too."

☆　☆　☆

The teacher handed out the test papers and told the children they could start answering the questions.

She noticed little Billy sitting with his head bowed, his hands over his face. She approached him.

"Don't you feel well?" she inquired.

"Oh, I'm fine, teacher. Maybe it's unconstitutional, but I always pray before a test!"

☆　☆　☆

A Presbyterian minister was about to baptize a

baby. Turning to the father, he inquired, "His name, please?"

"William Patrick Arthur Timothy John Mac-Arthur."

The minister turned to his assistant and said, "A little more water, please."

☆ ☆ ☆

A little boy excited about his part in the Christmas play came home and said:

"I got a part in the Christmas play!"

"What part?" asked his mother.

"I'm one of the three wise guys!" was the reply.

☆ ☆ ☆

St. Peter looked at the new arrival skeptically; he had no advance knowledge of his coming.

"How did you get here?" he asked.

"Flu."

☆ ☆ ☆

Two boys were trying to outdo each other. The first said, "My uncle's a doctor. I can be sick for nothing!" The second youngster shot back, "Big deal! My uncle is a preacher. I can be good for nothing!"

☆ ☆ ☆

"Mommy," said little Judy, "did you ever see a cross-eyed bear?"

"Why, no, Judy," chuckled her mother. "But why do you ask?"

"Well, in Sunday school this morning, we sang about 'the consecrated cross-eyed bear.' "

☆ ☆ ☆

The sermon was very long this Sunday morning and little Donny was getting more restless by the minute.

Suddenly, in a whisper too loud for his mother's comfort, he blurted out, "If we give him the money now, Ma, will he let us go out?"

☆   ☆   ☆

"Daddy, I want to ask you a question," said little Bobby after his first day in Sunday school.

"Yes, Bobby, what is it?"

"The teacher was reading the Bible to us—all about the children of Israel building the temple, the children of Israel crossing the Red Sea, the children of Israel making sacrifices. Didn't the grownups do anything?"

☆   ☆   ☆

The little young lady of the house, by way of punishment for some minor misdemeanor, was compelled to eat her dinner alone at a little table in a corner of the dining room. The rest of the family paid no attention to her presence until they heard her audibly praying over her repast with the words, "I thank thee, Lord, for preparing a table before me in the presence of mine enemies."

☆   ☆   ☆

People who cough incessantly never seem to go to a doctor—they go to banquets, concerts, and church.

☆   ☆   ☆

Did you hear about the man from the income tax bureau who phoned a certain Baptist minister to say, "We're checking the tax return of a member of your church, Deacon X., and notice he lists a donation to your building fund of three hundred dollars. Is that correct?" The minister answered without hesitation, "I haven't got my records available, but I'll promise you one thing: if he hasn't, he *will!*"

☆　☆　☆

The minister's little daughter was sent to bed with a stomach-ache and missed her usual romp with her daddy. A few minutes later she appeared at the top of the stairs and called to her mother, "Mama, let me talk with Daddy."

"No, my dear, not tonight. Get back in bed."

"Please, mama."

"I said 'no.' That's enough now."

"Mother, I'm a very sick woman, and I must see my pastor at once."

☆　☆　☆

A Mormon acquaintance once pushed Mark Twain into an argument on the issue of polygamy. After long and tedious expositions justifying the practice, the Mormon demanded that Twain cite any passage of Scripture expressly forbidding polygamy.

"Nothing easier," Twain replied. " 'No man can serve two masters.' "

☆　☆　☆

COLD CUTS

When I look at you, time stands still . . . what I really mean is that your face would stop a clock.

☆　☆　☆

He has a face like a saint . . . a Saint Bernard.

☆　☆　☆

She has a face that looks like it wore out six bodies.

☆　☆　☆

She's had so many face-lifting jobs, every time she raises her eyebrows, she pulls up her stockings.

☆　☆　☆

I'm really pleased to see you're back . . . particularly after seeing your face.

☆　☆　☆

Well, well, well . . . all dressed up and no face to go.

☆　☆　☆

I never forget a face, but in your case, I'm willing to make an exception.

☆　☆　☆

There are two things I don't like about you . . . your face!

☆　☆　☆

She has a nice, open face . . . open day and night.

☆　☆　☆

I don't recall your face but your breath is familiar!

☆　☆　☆

Your face is familiar . . . I just can't recall which museum!

☆　　☆　　☆

He should join the Ku Klux Klan—he'd look better with a hood over his face.

☆　　☆　　☆

The only way she can get color in her face is to stick her tongue out.

☆　　☆　　☆

He has a sympathetic face; it has everyone's sympathy.

☆　　☆　　☆

She's not exactly bad looking. There's just a little blemish between her ears . . . her face.

☆　　☆　　☆

Everyone says she's an angel fallen from the skies. Too bad she happened to land on her face.

☆　　☆　　☆

Her face was so wrinkled she didn't dare wear long earrings—made her look like a Venetian blind.

☆　　☆　　☆

Count to three; see if you can do it from memory.

☆　　☆　　☆

He has a small birthmark on his head . . . his brain.

☆　　☆　　☆

She looks like she had her face lifted and the crane broke.

☆   ☆   ☆

You must be a twin . . . no one person could be that stupid!

☆   ☆   ☆

I wish I had a lower I.Q. so I could enjoy your company.

☆   ☆   ☆

Why don't you pal around with a half-wit so you can have someone to look up to!

☆   ☆   ☆

His trouble is too much bone in the head and not enough in the back.

☆   ☆   ☆

He has a concrete mind . . . permanently set and all mixed up.

☆   ☆   ☆

He's a gross ignoramus . . . 144-times worse than an ordinary ignoramus.

☆   ☆   ☆

He's a man of rare intelligence . . . it's rare when he shows any.

☆   ☆   ☆

It's a mystery how his head grew without any nourishment.

☆　☆　☆

In your case, brain surgery would be a minor operation.

☆　☆　☆

What he lacks in intelligence he makes up in stupidity.

☆　☆　☆

You could make a fortune renting your head out as a balloon.

☆　☆　☆

I wouldn't fret so much if I were you . . . after all, we can't all be mentally sound.

☆　☆　☆

Look, I'm not going to engage in a battle of wits with you . . . I never attack anyone who's unarmed.

☆　☆　☆

The only reason he manages to keep his head above water is that wood floats.

☆　☆　☆

He's an M.D. . . . Mentally Deficient.

☆　☆　☆

Why don't you sue your brains for nonsupport?

☆　☆　☆

She was hurt while taking a milk bath. The cow slipped and fell on her head.

☆   ☆   ☆

I won't say she's narrow minded . . . but if it gets any worse she'll only have to use one earring.

☆   ☆   ☆

He has a lot of backbone. The trouble is, the bone is all on the top.

☆   ☆   ☆

You have a ready wit. Let me know when it's ready.

☆   ☆   ☆

He spends half his time trying to be witty. You might say he's a half-wit.

☆   ☆   ☆

He's going to the hospital for a minor operation . . . they're putting a brain in.

☆   ☆   ☆

My wife wants a vacuum for Christmas. Is your head available?

☆   ☆   ☆

The only reason we invited him here tonight is to remind you that every 60 seconds mental illness strikes!

☆   ☆   ☆

You know, if brains were dynamite, he wouldn't have enough to blow his nose!

☆　　☆　　☆

He's just as smart as he can be . . . unfortunately.

☆　　☆　　☆

You'll make money someday. Your ignorance is comical.

☆　　☆　　☆

He won't have to wait till he dies to be at his wit's end.

☆　　☆　　☆

What's on your mind? . . . if you'll please excuse the exaggeration.

☆　　☆　　☆

He should study to be a bone specialist. He has the head for it.

☆　　☆　　☆

You know, there's a reason he's always got that stupid grin on his face: he's *stupid!*

☆　　☆　　☆

He has an I.Q. just below plant life!

☆　　☆　　☆

Generally speaking, she's generally speaking.

☆　　☆　　☆

He has the awful flower disease . . . he's a blooming idiot!

☆　　☆　　☆

Your mind will stay young . . . you use it so little!

☆　　☆　　☆

He has a soft heart and a head to match!

☆　　☆　　☆

I'm paid to make an idiot out of myself. Why do you do it for free?

☆　　☆　　☆

He's not just an ordinary moron . . . he's a moron's moron.

☆　　☆　　☆

Her vocabulary is small, but the turnover is terrific.

☆　　☆　　☆

First thing in the morning, she brushes her teeth and sharpens her tongue.

☆　　☆　　☆

She belongs to the meddle class.

☆　　☆　　☆

She has a keen sense of rumor.

☆　　☆　　☆

Listening to him makes you think of a river . . . small at the head and big at the mouth.

☆ ☆ ☆

He must have goat glands . . . he's always butting in.

☆ ☆ ☆

How can you talk all night without stopping to think?

☆ ☆ ☆

He is the only person who enters the room mouth first!

☆ ☆ ☆

If exercise eliminates fat, how in theworld did you get that double chin?

☆ ☆ ☆

You really have an open mind . . . and a mouth to match.

☆ ☆ ☆

He carries pictures of the children and a sound track of his wife.

☆ ☆ ☆

You could make a fortune if you could buy him for what you think of him and sell him for what he thinks of himself.

☆ ☆ ☆

Their marriage is a partnership . . . he's the silent partner.

☆　　☆　　☆

He's a second-story man; no one ever believes his first story.

☆　　☆　　☆

He has such a big mouth he can eat a banana sideways, or sing duets by himself.

☆　　☆　　☆

He sure has got a wide mouth for such a narrow mind.

☆　　☆　　☆

Arguing with her is like trying to read a newspaper in a high wind.

☆　　☆　　☆

Can she talk! She was in Miami and when she got home her tongue was sunburned.

☆　　☆　　☆

When he meets another egotist, it's an I for an I.

☆　　☆　　☆

He's always down on everything he's not up on.

☆　　☆　　☆

He's an I-sore.

☆　　☆　　☆

English is the mother tongue . . . because father seldom has a chance to use it.

☆　　☆　　☆

She has a good memory—and a tongue hung in the middle of it.

☆　　☆　　☆

Her tongue is so long she can seal an envelope after she puts it in the mailbox.

☆　　☆　　☆

They call her "A.T. & T." . . . Always Talking and Talking.

☆　　☆　　☆

She's so tired at the end of the day she can hardly keep her mouth open.

☆　　☆　　☆

On his last birthday he sent his parents a telegram of congratulations.

☆　　☆　　☆

He's suffering from I-dolatry.

☆　　☆　　☆

If he had his life to live over again, he would still fall in love with himself.

☆　　☆　　☆

He doesn't want anyone to make a fuss over him

... just to treat him as they would any other great man.

☆　☆　☆

She has such a sour look that when she puts on face cream it curdles.

☆　☆　☆

She only has to go to the dentist twice a year ... once for each tooth.

☆　☆　☆

Be careful when you're speaking about him ... you're speaking of the man he loves.

☆　☆　☆

Someone should press the "down" button on his elevator shoes.

☆　☆　☆

She's tried to get a man ... but without avail— maybe she'd better wear one.

☆　☆　☆

Tell me, is that your lower lip, or are you wearing a turtleneck sweater?

☆　☆　☆

Every girl has the right to be ugly, but she abused the privilege.

☆　☆　☆

She will never live to be as old as she looks.

☆　☆　☆

She looks like a million . . . every year of it.

☆　☆　☆

She has black hair and nails to match.

☆　☆　☆

She has long flowing blond hair . . . from each nostril.

☆　☆　☆

Did you notice her cute little nose . . . the way it turned up, then down, then sideways?

☆　☆　☆

She looks like a professional blind date.

☆　☆　☆

His left eye was so fascinating that his right eye kept looking at it all the time.

☆　☆　☆

Is that your head, or did your body blow a bubble?

☆　☆　☆

She has everything a man would desire—including heft, bulging muscles, and a moustache.

☆　☆　☆

The only thing that can make her look good is distance.

☆　　☆　　☆

Her nostrils are so big that when you kiss her it's like driving into a two-car garage.

☆　　☆　　☆

Is that your nose, or are you eating a banana?

☆　　☆　　☆

She has early American features . . . she looks like a buffalo.

☆　　☆　　☆

Her hat looks as if it had made a forced landing on her head.

☆　　☆　　☆

She has worn that dress so many years it's been in style five times.

☆　　☆　　☆

Sit down; you make the place look shabby!

☆　　☆　　☆

He dresses like an unmade bed!

☆　　☆　　☆

That dress she's wearing will never go out of style . . . it will look just as ridiculous year after year.

☆　　☆　　☆

She has absolutely nothing to wear—and three closets to keep it in.

☆   ☆   ☆

She says that whenever she's down in the dumps she gets a new hat . . . I thought all along that's where she gets them.

☆   ☆   ☆

You were here last year, weren't you? I never forget a dress!

☆   ☆   ☆

You know, mister, you have some very funny material . . . in your suit!

☆   ☆   ☆

Don't try and judge her by her clothes . . . there isn't enough evidence.

☆   ☆   ☆

That's a very cute dress she almost has on.

☆   ☆   ☆

After they made him they broke the jelly mold.

☆   ☆   ☆

He has a great labor-saving device . . . tomorrow.

☆   ☆   ☆

He's a regular Rock of Jello.

☆   ☆   ☆

She has a suit for every day in the month . . . the one she has on.

☆　☆　☆

Her clothes look as though she'd dressed in front of an airplane propeller.

☆　☆　☆

He's never been married . . . he's a self-made mouse.

☆　☆　☆

He is so nervous that he keeps coffee awake.

☆　☆　☆

He's the real decisive type . . . he'll give you a definite "maybe."

☆　☆　☆

They call him "Jigsaw." Every time he's faced with a problem he goes to pieces.

☆　☆　☆

Pardon my bluntness, but would you please stand down wind!

☆　☆　☆

She's a vision . . . a real sight.

☆　☆　☆

After her wedding everybody kissed the groom.

☆　☆　☆

When she comes into a room the mice jump on chairs.

☆ ☆ ☆

She's so ugly that when she goes to the beach the tide won't come in.

☆ ☆ ☆

His breath was so bad that his dentist had to work on his teeth through his ear.

☆ ☆ ☆

He's a good argument for evolution . . . the missing link!

☆ ☆ ☆

Whatever is eating him must be suffering from indigestion.

☆ ☆ ☆

He's a contact man . . . all con and no tact.

☆ ☆ ☆

If he had his conscience taken out, it would be a minor operation.

☆ ☆ ☆

She put her makeup on with a paint roller.

☆ ☆ ☆

In the etiquette class he once attended, he was unanimously voted the student most likely to return.

☆ ☆ ☆

I once saw a movie that was so bad six states use it in place of capital punishment.

☆　☆　☆

He left his job because of illness and fatigue . . . his boss got sick and tired of him.

☆　☆　☆

The only thing he's ever achieved on his own is dandruff.

☆　☆　☆

Why don't you get yourself X-rayed to see what people see in you.

☆　☆　☆

Next time you pass my house I'll appreciate it.

☆　☆　☆

When he was born, the doctor called him, "Theophilus" . . . he's theophilus baby I have ever seen.

☆　☆　☆

They call him "Coliseum" . . . he's a monumental ruin.

☆　☆　☆

You've heard of the March of Time? This is his brother, Waste of Time!

☆　☆　☆

Anything goes tonight and you may be the first.

☆　☆　☆

He's full of brotherly love; he always stops anyone who's beating a donkey.

☆　　☆　　☆

Was the ground cold when you crawled out this morning?

☆　　☆　　☆

She has the knack of making strangers immediately.

☆　　☆　　☆

Just because you're a Democrat doesn't mean you're odd or obnoxious . . . stupid, maybe, but not odd or obnoxious.

☆　　☆　　☆

That's okay, folks . . . let him have his fun tonight. Tomorrow he'll be back on the garbage truck.

☆　　☆　　☆

I understand when you were a kid your mother sent your picture to Ripley and it was promptly returned, marked, "I don't believe it!"

☆　　☆　　☆

Let me just say, I've seen more excitement at the opening of an umbrella.

☆　　☆　　☆

Let me sum up this motion picture by saying, I've seen better film on teeth!

☆　　☆　　☆

I remember you . . . you're a graduate of the Don
Rickles Charm School!

☆　　☆　　☆

That's very good. We ought to team up and do a
single!

☆　　☆　　☆

Some cause happiness wherever they go; others,
whenever they go.

☆　　☆　　☆

He says he'd only marry a girl who can take a
joke . . . that's the only kind who would take him.

☆　　☆　　☆

Listen, baboon, don't accuse me of making a monkey out of you; why should I take all the credit?

☆　　☆　　☆

He's the kind of guy that can really creep into
your heart and mind. In fact, you'll never meet a
bigger creep!

☆　　☆　　☆

He looks like his mother was frightened by everything!

☆　　☆　　☆

When he was two, his family moved. But he found
them again!

☆　　☆　　☆

73

Put your hand in front of your mouth when you sneeze. It keeps your teeth from flying out.

☆　☆　☆

It may just be morbid curiosity, but I would like to see your parents!

☆　☆　☆

When she goes down to the waterfront, even the tugboats stop whistling.

☆　☆　☆

He had to see his doctor in the morning for a blood test, so he stayed up all night studying for it.

☆　☆　☆

At a holiday party, they hung her and kissed the mistletoe.

☆　☆　☆

Guys like him don't grow on trees . . . they swing from them!

☆　☆　☆

He's a college man. You've heard of the rambling wrecks from Georgia Tech? Well, he's sort of a total loss from Holy Cross.

☆　☆　☆

Someday he'll be arrested for impersonating a human being!

☆　☆　☆

She has delusions of glamour!

☆　☆　☆

And just when did you fall out of the hearse?

☆　☆　☆

They say success is 90 percent perspiration—you must be a *tremendous* success!

☆　☆　☆

It's not the ups and downs in life that bother me, it's the jerks like you.

☆　☆　☆

He's one person who would make a perfect stranger!

☆　☆　☆

Stay with me . . . I want to be alone.

☆　☆　☆

For a minute I didn't recognize you. It was my most enjoyable minute today.

☆　☆　☆

Don't go away . . . I want to forget you exactly as you are.

☆　☆　☆

If you were alive, you'd be a very sick man.

☆　☆　☆

At almost every party his wife is sure to be asked by someone, "What does your husband want to be when he grows up?"

☆   ☆   ☆

There are people who are liked wherever they go; he's only liked whenever he goes.

☆   ☆   ☆

When he leaves a party the guests know the meaning of comic relief.

☆   ☆   ☆

They call him "garbage man" . . . he has a certain air about him.

☆   ☆   ☆

You remind me of some of those dances . . . one, two, three, jerk!

☆   ☆   ☆

I'd like to say we're glad you're here. I'd like to say it.

☆   ☆   ☆

I'll bet your parents hit the jerkpot.

☆   ☆   ☆

My son was annoying me the other morning, so I said, "Why don't you go out and play on the freeway?"

☆   ☆   ☆

I remember the day I had a wreck in my car. Six months later I married her.

I had a girl that got so tan in the summer that I gave her a very practical birthday gift . . . saddle soap.

She can't cook or clean but she can lick her weight in trading stamps.

She made him a millionaire. Before she married him, he was a billionaire.

I was invited up to Judy's place for dinner last night. I don't want to say she's a bad housekeeper, but you wipe your feet after you leave.

He can stay longer in an hour than most people do in a week.

When it comes to telling her age, she's shy . . . about ten years shy.

He's a great athlete . . . he can throw a wet blanket the entire length of a room.

He's a man of promise ... broken promise.

☆ ☆ ☆

He lights up a room when he leaves it.

☆ ☆ ☆

There's no doubt he's trying ... in fact, he's very trying.

☆ ☆ ☆

He's very cultured ... he can bore you on any subject.

☆ ☆ ☆

He sent his picture to the Lonely Hearts Club. The reply came back, "We're not that lonely."

☆ ☆ ☆

There's a bus leaving in ten minutes ... be under it!

☆ ☆ ☆

She's a rag, a bone, and a hank of hair ... and he's a brag, a groan, and a tank of air.

☆ ☆ ☆

He stopped drinking coffee in the morning because it keeps him awake the rest of the day.

☆ ☆ ☆

She's not completely useless: five charm schools are using her as a bad example.

☆ ☆ ☆

He's a real big gun ... of small caliber and immense bore.

☆ ☆ ☆

Don't tell me ... I know who you are. You're the reason for birth control.

☆ ☆ ☆

I understand you throw yourself into everything you undertake; please go and dig a deep well.

☆ ☆ ☆

They call her "Appendix" ... if you take her out once, that's enough.

☆ ☆ ☆

He's mean, selfish, loudmouthed, and uncouth, but in spite of all that there's something about him that repels you.

☆ ☆ ☆

He claims he used to be an organist but gave it up ... his monkey must have died.

☆ ☆ ☆

He's such a phony that he gets cavities in his false teeth.

☆ ☆ ☆

He was a born mountaineer and hasn't been on the level since.

☆ ☆ ☆

She's so contrary that if she drowned they'd look upstream for her.

☆ ☆ ☆

EDUCATION

A wise schoolteacher sends this note to all parents on the first day of school: "If you promise not to believe everything your child says happens at school, I'll promise not to believe everything he says happens at home."

☆ ☆ ☆

Teacher: "What are you—animal, vegetable or mineral?"

Little boy: "Vegetable. I am a human bean!"

☆ ☆ ☆

Tony: "My college has turned out some great men."

Daisy: "I didn't know you were a college graduate."

Tony: "I'm one they turned out!"

☆ ☆ ☆

It was the little girl's first day at school and the teacher was making out her registration card.

"What is your father's name?"

"Daddy," replied the child.

"Yes, I know, but what does your mother call him?"

"Oh, she doesn't call him anything. She likes him!"

☆　　☆　　☆

Teacher: "Why don't you brush your teeth? I can see what you had for breakfast this morning."
Student: "What did I have?"
Teacher: "Eggs!"
Student: "You're wrong! That was yesterday!"

☆　　☆　　☆

A college education seldom hurts a man if he is willing to learn a little something after he graduates.

☆　　☆　　☆

Girl: "Too bad you flunked the test. How far were you from the right answer?"
Boy: "Two seats!"

☆　　☆　　☆

A young college student had stayed up all night studying for his zoology test the next day. As he entered the classroom, he saw ten stands with ten birds on them with a sack over each bird and only the legs showing. He sat right on the front row because he wanted to do the best job possible. The professor announced that the test would be to look at each of the birds' legs and give the common name, habitat, genus, species, etc.

The student looked at each of the birds' legs. They all looked the same to him. He began to get upset. He had stayed up all night studying and now had to identify birds by their legs. The more he thought about it the madder he got. Finally, he could stand it no longer. He went up to the professor's desk and said, "What a stupid test! How could anyone tell the difference of birds by looking at their legs?" With that the student threw his test on the professor's desk and walked to the door.

The professor was surprised. The class was so big that he didn't know every student's name so as the student reached the door the professor called, "Mister, what's your name!"

The enraged student pulled up his pant legs and said, "You guess, buddy! You guess!"

☆ ☆ ☆

A father was examining his son's report card. "One thing is definitely in your favor," he announced. "With this report card, you couldn't possibly be cheating."

☆ ☆ ☆

There's one great thing to be said for a college education. It enables you to worry about things all over the world.

☆ ☆ ☆

College student with coin in hand: "If it's heads, I go to bed. If it's tails, I stay up. If it stands on edge, I study."

☆ ☆ ☆

The quickest way for a child to get attention in school these days is for him to bend his IBM card.

☆ ☆ ☆

Professor: "If there are any dumbbells in the room, please stand up."

(There was a long pause, then a lone freshman

stood up in the rear.) "What? Do you consider your-self a dumbbell?"

Freshman: "Well, not exactly, but I hate to see you standing all alone."

☆　☆　☆

Teacher: "Johnny, give me a sentence with a direct object."

Johnny: "Teacher, everybody thinks you're beautiful."

Teacher: "Thank you, Johnny, but what is the object?"

Johnny: "A good report card."

☆　☆　☆

In explaining her tardiness to English class, a high-school junior stated demurely, "The boy who was following me walked very slowly."

☆　☆　☆

Teacher: "If your mother gave you a large apple and a small one, and told you to divide with your brother, which would you give him?"

Johnnie: "Do you mean my little brother or my big brother?"

☆　☆　☆

For weeks a six-year-old lad kept telling his first-grade teacher about the baby brother or sister that was expected at his house. Then one day the mother allowed the boy to feel the movements of the unborn child. The six-year-old was obviously impressed, but made no comment. Furthermore, he stopped telling his teacher about the impending event. The teacher finally sat the boy on her lap and said, "Tommy, whatever has become of that baby brother or sister you were expecting at home?" Tommy burst into tears and confessed, "I think Mommie ate it!"

☆ ☆ ☆

Librarian: "Please be quiet. The people next to you can't read."

Boy: "What a shame! I've been reading since I was six."

☆ ☆ ☆

Teacher: "Billy, what did you do when Ed called you a liar?"

Billy: "I remembered what you told me: 'A soft answer turns away anger.'"

Teacher: "Very good, Billy. What answer did you give him?"

Billy: "I answered him with a soft tomato."

☆ ☆ ☆

Teacher: "Really, Tommy, your handwriting is terrible! You must learn to write better."

Tommy: "Well, if I did, you'd be finding fault with my spelling."

☆ ☆ ☆

Teacher: "What is an emperor?"

Scholar: "I don't know."

Teacher: "An emperor is a ruler."

Scholar: "Oh, sure; I used to carry an emperor to school with me."

☆ ☆ ☆

"Some plants," said the teacher, "have the prefix 'dog.' For instance, there is the dogrose, the dogwood, the dogviolet. Who can name another plant prefixed by 'dog?'

"I can," shouted a little boy in the back row. "Collie flower."

☆ ☆ ☆

As a special treat, a teacher took her class to visit the museum of natural history. The children returned home excitedly, and on rushing into his house one of the little boys greeted his mother exuberantly: "What do you think we did today, Mother? The teacher took us to a dead circus."

☆ ☆ ☆

Interrupted by the sound of the bell announcing the end of the class, the professor was annoyed to see the students noisily preparing to leave although he was in the middle of his lecture. "Just a moment, gentlemen," he said, "I have a few more pearls to cast."

☆ ☆ ☆

Teacher: "Johnny, how much is three times three?"

Johnny: "Nine."

Teacher: "That's pretty good."

Johnny: "Pretty good? Say, 'it's perfect.'"

☆ ☆ ☆

He was in school so long the other pupils used to bring him apples thinking he was the teacher.

☆ ☆ ☆

Sometimes you wonder what kids are really learning. Yesterday a teacher pointed at the flag, turned to my six-year-old and asked him what it was. He answers, "It is the flag of my country!" The teacher couldn't leave well enough alone. She said, "Now tell me the name of your country." And he says, " 'Tis of thee!"

☆　☆　☆

Teacher: "I hope I didn't see you looking at someone else's paper, Billy."
Billy: "I hope so, too, Teacher."

☆　☆　☆

Student: "I don't think I deserve a zero on this test!"
Teacher: "Neither do I, but it's the lowest mark I can give you."

☆　☆　☆

College boy to his mother, "I decided that I want to be a political science major and that I want to clean up the mess in the world!"
"That's very nice," purred his mother. "You can go upstairs and start with your room."

☆　☆　☆

A student wrote the following on his pre-Christmas examination paper: "God only knows the answer to this question. Merry Christmas!"
The professor returned the paper with the following notation: "God gets an 'A'; you get an 'F'. Happy New Year!"

☆　☆　☆

Teacher: "Where's your homework this morning?"
Student: "You'll never believe this, but on the

way to school I made a paper airplane out of it and someone hijacked it to Cuba!"

☆ ☆ ☆

FOOD

A man walked into a restaurant in a strange town. The waiter came and asked him for his order. Feeling lonely, he replied, "Meat loaf and a kind word." When the waiter returned with the meat loaf, the man said, "Where's the good word?" The waiter put down the meat loaf and sighed, bent down and whispered, "Don't eat the meat loaf."

☆ ☆ ☆

Cook: "Do you want me to cut this pizza into six or eight pieces?"
Man: "You'd better make it six . . . I don't think I can eat eight pieces!"

☆ ☆ ☆

Customer: "Do you serve crabs in this dump?"
Waiter: "Yes, sir; what'll you have?"

☆ ☆ ☆

"Waiter!" shouted an irate customer. "I can't tell whether this is coffee or tea! It tastes like benzine!"·
"If it tastes like benzine then it positively is coffee," the waiter said. "Our tea tastes like turpentine."

☆ ☆ ☆

"Waiter," said the surprised customer as he examined his check, "what's this eight dollars for?"

"For the chopped liver sandwich, sir."

"Yeah?" The customer nodded. "Whose liver was it? Rockefeller's?"

☆　☆　☆

The manager of a restaurant called his waitresses together. "Girls," he began, "I want you all to look your best today. Greet every customer with a smile, put on a little extra makeup, and see to it that your hair is in place."

"What's up?" asked one of the girls. "Bunch of big shots coming in today?"

"No, the meat's tough today."

☆　☆　☆

Waiter: "How's the soup, sir?"

Diner: "To tell you the truth, I'm really sorry I stirred it."

☆　☆　☆

Customer: "Those franks you sold me were meat at one end and corn meal at the other!"

Butcher: "Yes, ma'am; in these times it's difficult to make both ends meat."

☆　☆　☆

Man: "I can't eat this food! Call the manager!"

Waitress: "It's no use, sir. He can't eat it either."

☆　☆　☆

A meek little man in a restaurant timidly touched the arm of a man putting on an overcoat. "Excuse me," he said, "but do you happen to be Mr. Smith of Newport?"

"No, I'm not!" the man answered impatiently.

"Oh-er-well," stammered the first man, "you see, I am, and that's his overcoat you're putting on."

☆　☆　☆

Sign in restaurant: "Our customers are always right: misinformed, perhaps, inexact, bullheaded, fickle, even downright stupid, but never wrong."

☆　☆　☆

Joe: "A panhandler came up to me and said he hadn't had a bite in two weeks."

Moe: "Poor fellow. What did you do?"

Joe: "Bit him, of course!"

☆　☆　☆

I know a woman who has cooked so many TV dinners she thinks she's in show business.

☆　☆　☆

Man: "Do you serve breakfast here?"

Waitress: "Sure; what'll it be?"

Man: "Let me have watery scrambled eggs . . . and some burnt toast . . . and some weak coffee, lukewarm."

Waitress: "Whatever you say, sir."

Man: "Now, are you doing anything while that order is going through?"

Waitress: "Why—no, sir."

Man: "Then sit here and nag me awhile . . . I'm homesick!"

☆　☆　☆

I hate to always eat and run, but the way I tip it's the only safe procedure.

☆ ☆ ☆

Customer: "Your sign says, '$50 to anyone who orders something we can't furnish.' I would like to have an elephant ear sandwich."

Waiter: "Ohhh . . . we're going to have to pay you the $50."

Customer: "No elephant ears, huh?"

Waiter: "Oh, we've got lots of them . . . but we're all out of those big buns!"

☆ ☆ ☆

McTavish: "A fellow walked up to me today and asked for a nickel for a cup of coffee. I gave it to him and then followed him clear across town to the restaurant."

☆ ☆ ☆

Customer: "What flavors of ice cream do you have?"

Hoarse waitress: "Vanilla, strawberry, and chocolate."

Customer: "Do you have laryngitis?"

Waitress: "No; just vanilla, strawberry, and chocolate."

☆ ☆ ☆

Shopper: "The way food prices are going up, it soon will be cheaper to eat the money."

☆ ☆ ☆

Diner: "What would you recommend for tonight?"

Waiter: "Go someplace else . . . the cook is on strike."

☆   ☆   ☆

Percy: "I won't criticize their chef, but you'll notice three shakers on every table . . . salt, pepper, and Alka-Seltzer."

☆   ☆   ☆

Waiter: "Would you like your coffee black?"
Customer: "What other colors do you have?"

☆   ☆   ☆

Diner: "What's this fly doing in my soup?"
Waiter: "The back stroke."

☆   ☆   ☆

Customer: "Waitress, why is my doughnut all smashed?"
Waitress: "You said you wanted a cup of coffee and a doughnut, and step on it."

☆   ☆   ☆

Customer: "Your sign says you will cook any type of steak? I'll try an elephant steak."
Waiter: "Will that be African or Indian?"

☆   ☆   ☆

Waiter: "And how did you find your steak, sir?"
Customer: "I just lifted one of the brussel sprouts and there it was!"

☆   ☆   ☆

Customer: "This food isn't fit for a pig!"
Waiter: "I'm sorry, sir. I'll bring you some that is."

☆　☆　☆

Tim: "Look, Jim, why are you always trying to impress me? So you spoke to the waiter in French! So, big deal! So what good is it to know French? . . . What did he tell you, waiter?"
Waiter: "He told me to give you the check, sir!"

☆　☆　☆

Customer: "Your sign says, "Any sandwich you can name." I would like a whale sandwich."
Waiter: "Okay. (Disappears into kitchen and shortly returns.) I'm afraid I can't get you a whale sandwich."
Customer: "Why not? . . . your sign says "any sandwich."
Waiter: "The cook says he doesn't want to start a new whale for one lousy sandwich."

☆　☆　☆

GETTING OLDER

Middle age is when you know all the answers and nobody asks you the questions.

☆　☆　☆

Three stages of man: Youth; Middle age; "You're looking fine."

☆　☆　☆

Forty is the age when a woman stops patting herself on the back and begins on the chin.

☆ ☆ ☆

There are three ways to tell if you are getting old: first, a loss of memory; second, . . .

☆ ☆ ☆

The hardest decision in life is when to start middle age.

☆ ☆ ☆

Middle age is when the narrow waist and the broad mind begin to change places.

☆ ☆ ☆

GOLF

Bill: "I'd move heaven and earth to break my 110 score."

Phil: "Try moving heaven. You've already moved plenty of earth today."

☆ ☆ ☆

Caddy: "Let me say this about your game, mister. I wouldn't say you were the *worst* golfer I have ever seen on this course, but I've seen places today that I've never seen before."

☆ ☆ ☆

"Look," the golfer screamed at his caddy, "if you

don't keep your big mouth shut, you'll drive me out of my mind."

"That's no drive, mister," corrected the caddy. "That's a putt."

☆ ☆ ☆

Golfer: "Notice any improvement since last year?"
Caddy: "Polished your clubs, didn't you?"

☆ ☆ ☆

Golfer: "Why do you keep looking at your watch?"
Caddy: "This isn't a watch, sir. It's a compass!"

☆ ☆ ☆

Golfer: "The doctor says I can't play golf."
Caddy: "Ah, he's played with you, too, huh?"

☆ ☆ ☆

"Caddy, why didn't you see where that ball went?"

"Well, it doesn't usually go anywhere, Mr. Smith. You got me off guard."

☆ ☆ ☆

The other day I was playing golf and saw an unusual thing. A golfer became so mad that he threw his brand new set of golf clubs into the lake. A few minutes later he came back, waded into the lake and retrieved his clubs. He proceeded to take his car keys out of the bag and then threw the clubs back into the water.

☆ ☆ ☆

Golfer: "Well, what do you think of my game?"
Caddy: "I guess it's all right, but I still like golf better."

☆　☆　☆

Golfer: "How would you have played that last shot, caddy?"
Caddy: "Under an assumed name!"

☆　☆　☆

Golfer: "You must be the world's worst caddy!"
Caddy: "No, sir! That would be too much of a coincidence!"

☆　☆　☆

HEAVY, HEAVY

"He is suffering from Dunlaps' disease."
"What is Dunlaps' disease?"
"His stomach done-laps over his belt!"

☆　☆　☆

He was so fat during his school days that everytime he would get up and turn around he would erase the blackboard.

☆　☆　☆

She was so fat that she even had a shadow at high noon.

☆　☆　☆

She was so big that everyone in the classroom at school sat next to her.

☆　☆　☆

"I just lost ten pounds!"
"Turn around; I think I found them!"

☆　☆　☆

If he's not overweight, then he's certainly six inches too short.

☆　☆　☆

He has T.B.—Twin Bellies.

☆　☆　☆

He's a do-it-yourself man. He made a bay window with a knife and fork.

☆　☆　☆

Lately he's tried tranquilizers to reduce. He hasn't lost any weight, but he has stopped worrying about being beefy and paunchy.

☆　☆　☆

He's on a garlic diet. He hasn't lost any weight, but quite a few friends.

☆　☆　☆

(Wife to husband that just got off the scale) "Your fortune says that you are handsome, debonair, and wealthy. It even has your weight wrong!"

☆　☆　☆

He's not only a heavy but a fast eater. He starts on his dessert before the echo of his soup has died away.

☆   ☆   ☆

He has so many chins, he should be careful not to burp . . . it would start a ripple.

☆   ☆   ☆

When she got married, they threw puffed rice.

☆   ☆   ☆

She had mumps for five days and no one knew it.

☆   ☆   ☆

He was so fat that when he stepped on a penny scale the card came out and said, "ONE AT A TIME, PLEASE!"

☆   ☆   ☆

My wife is on a diet . . . coconuts and bananas. She hasn't lost any weight, but, boy, can she climb a tree!

☆   ☆   ☆

When she jogs around the block, everything is jogging except her feet.

☆   ☆   ☆

It's not her fault that she's heavy. It's her glands . . . they weigh two hundred pounds.

☆   ☆   ☆

I wonder why it is that fat men are always good

natured? Probably because it takes them so long to get mad clear through.

☆ ☆ ☆

Putting on weight is the penalty for exceeding the feed limit.

☆ ☆ ☆

When she gets the hiccups in her bathing suit . . . it looks like somebody adjusting a venetian blind.

☆ ☆ ☆

She weighs one hundred and plenty.

☆ ☆ ☆

He's so fat, when he falls down he rocks himself to sleep trying to get up.

☆ ☆ ☆

She eats so much they use her picture on food-stamps.

☆ ☆ ☆

"You ran me down! Why couldn't you have driven around me?"
"I didn't think I had enough gas."

☆ ☆ ☆

He's living 'way beyond his seams.

☆ ☆ ☆

Trying hard to get on a bus, she snapped to the

man in back of her, "If you were half a man, you'd help me onto this bus." He answered, "If you were half a lady, you wouldn't need any help."

☆　☆　☆

The only sure way to reduce is to set the bathroom scale in front of the refrigerator.

☆　☆　☆

The worst kind of reducing pill is the one who keeps telling you how he did it.

☆　☆　☆

She's a perfect model . . . for a shipbuilder.

☆　☆　☆

His wife got rid of 235 pounds of ugly fat . . . she divorced him.

☆　☆　☆

Have you ever considered No-Cal shampoo? It's especially made for fatheads.

☆　☆　☆

Lem: "Do you know what the man got who invented Metrecal?"
Slim: "No, what?"
Lem: "The no-belly prize."

☆　☆　☆

He can sit around a table all by himself.

☆　☆　☆

My girlfriend weighs 500 pounds . . . she isn't fat but, boy, is she ever tall!

☆   ☆   ☆

I knew a guy in school that was so fat he sat in the first two rows!

☆   ☆   ☆

Visitor: "What will you do, dear, when you are as big as your mother?"
Little girl: "Diet."

☆   ☆   ☆

One good thing you can say for his obesity is that a great deal of him is having a good time.

☆   ☆   ☆

A sure-fire way to lose ten ugly pounds . . . cut off your head!

☆   ☆   ☆

There is one thing bigger than his stomach . . . his appetite.

☆   ☆   ☆

She: "I've got a new diet that is guaranteed to make you lose weight . . . and you can eat anything you want."
He: "You mean eat anything I want?"
She: "Yes, but don't swallow."

☆   ☆   ☆

A penny scale dispensed the following fortune

card to a fat lady, "You are very fond of food. You lack will power and you overdo everything. Either that or a baby elephant has just collapsed on this scale."

☆　☆　☆

He is so fat he can take a shower without getting his feet wet.

☆　☆　☆

He was so big he could apply for group insurance.

☆　☆　☆

For the past two weeks she's been doing a lot of horseback riding, and she's taken off ten pounds ... from the horse.

☆　☆　☆

IT'S ALL IN THE FAMILY

Advice to mothers: Unless you deliberately set aside a little time for regular relaxation, you will not be able to efficiently care for your family. Therefore, plan to relax a minimum of an hour and a half every fifteen years.

☆　☆　☆

These children are nuts today. I have a child myself, ten years old. He's going to be eleven ... if I let him!

☆　☆　☆

One day Johnny's father brought his boss home for dinner. When Johnny's mother served the meat, the little boy asked, "Is this mutton?" His mother replied, "No. Why do you ask?" "Because Dad said he was going to bring home a muttonhead for dinner," Johnny answered.

☆　　☆　　☆

Did you hear about the man who went behind the barn the night before Christmas, fired a shot, and then told his two children Santa Claus had committed suicide?

☆　　☆　　☆

Adolescence is a period of rapid changes. Between the ages of twelve and seventeen, for example, a child may see his parent age twenty years.

☆　　☆　　☆

After dinner, members of a lot of families suffer from dish-temper.

☆　　☆　　☆

The prevalence of juvenile delinquency is proving that parents are not getting at the seat of the problem.

☆　　☆　　☆

Mother: "Why did you fall in the mud puddle with your new dress on?"
Sally: "There wasn't time to take it off."

☆　　☆　　☆

Father: "What's wrong, Judy? Usually you talk on

the phone for hours. This time you only talked half an hour. How come?"

Judy: "It was the wrong number."

☆　☆　☆

A father, whose looks are not such as to warrant the breaking up of all existing statues of Apollo, tells this on himself:

My little girl was sitting on my lap facing a mirror. After gazing intently at her reflection for some minutes, she said, "Daddy, did God make you?"

"Certainly, my dear," I told her.

"And did he make me, too?" taking another look in the mirror.

"Certainly, dear. What makes you ask?"

"Seems to me He's doing better work lately."

☆　☆　☆

A letter from a college student, "Please send food packages! All they serve here is breakfast, lunch and dinner."

☆　☆　☆

Mother: "Aunt Mathilda won't kiss you with that dirty face."

Boy: "That's what I figured."

☆　☆　☆

"Dear Dad: Let me hear from you more often, even if it's only five or ten."

☆　☆　☆

"In our family," a little girl told her teacher, "everybody marries relatives. My father married my mother, my uncle married my aunt, and the other day I found that my grandmother married my grandfather."

☆ ☆ ☆

Father: "Well, son, what did you learn in school today?"

Son: "I learned to say, 'Yes, sir,' and 'No, sir,' and 'No, ma'am,' and 'Yes, ma'am.'"

Father: "Really?"

Son: "Yeah!"

☆ ☆ ☆

Nowadays you'll find almost everything in the average American home . . . except the family.

☆ ☆ ☆

Father of teen-age son to neighbor: "Junior's at that awkward age . . . too old for a spanking and too young for analysis."

☆ ☆ ☆

Son: "Dad, the Bible says if you don't let me have the car, you hate me."

Father: "Where does it say that?"

Son: "Proverbs 13:24—'He that spareth the rod hateth his son.'"

☆ ☆ ☆

Neighbor: "What is your son taking up at college?"

Father: "Space!"

☆ ☆ ☆

Husband: "It must be time to get up."

Wife: "How can you tell?"
Husband: "The baby has fallen asleep at last."

☆   ☆   ☆

Coed: "Daddy, the girl who sits next to me in class has a dress just like mine."
Dad: "So you want a new dress."
Coed: "Well, it would be cheaper than changing colleges."

☆   ☆   ☆

Jed: "Your sister is spoiled, isn't she?"
Ted: "No, that's the perfume she uses."

☆   ☆   ☆

Billy was in a store with his mother when he was given a stick of candy by one of the clerks.
"What do you say, Billy?" said his mother.
"Charge it!" he replied.

☆   ☆   ☆

Teen-age daughter (as the radio ground out the final notes of the latest hit song): "Did you ever hear anything so wonderful?"
Father: "Only once when a truck loaded with empty milk cans bumped another truck filled with live ducks."

☆   ☆   ☆

The mother said firmly, "If you two boys can't agree and be quiet, I shall take your pie away."
The younger one replied, "But, Mother, we do agree; Bill wants the biggest piece, and so do I!"

☆   ☆   ☆

Mother: "Eat your spinach. It will put color in your cheeks."

Son: "Who wants green cheeks?"

☆ ☆ ☆

There was an earthquake recently which frightened inhabitants of a certain town. One couple sent their little boy to stay with an uncle in another district, explaining the reason for the nephew's sudden visit. A day later the parents received this telegram, "Am returning your boy. Send the earthquake."

☆ ☆ ☆

Johnny: "Will I get everything I pray for, Mama?"

Mother: "Everything that's good for you, dear."

Johnny: "Oh, what's the use, then? I get that anyway."

☆ ☆ ☆

"Mother, do give me another piece of sugar," said little Helen.

"But you've had three already," her mother pointed out.

"Just one more, please."

"Well, this must be the last."

"Thank you, Mother . . . but I must say, you have no will power."

☆ ☆ ☆

Auntie: "When I was a child, I was told if I made ugly faces I would stay like it."

Little Joan: "Well, you can't say you weren't warned, Auntie."

☆ ☆ ☆

Little boy to departing relative, "There's no hurry, Auntie. Daddy has put the clock a whole hour ahead."

☆　☆　☆

Bobby had been to a birthday party, and, knowing his weakness, his mother looked him straight in the eye and said, "I hope you didn't ask for a second piece of cake."

"No," replied Bobby. "I only asked Mrs. Jones for the recipe so you could make some like it and she gave me two more pieces just of her own accord."

☆　☆　☆

Little boy (calling father at office): "Hello, who is this?"

Father (recognizing son's voice): "The smartest man in the world."

Little boy: "Pardon me; I got the wrong number."

☆　☆　☆

Father: "Can you support her in the way she's been accustomed to?"

Prospective son-in-law: "No, perhaps I cannot support her in the manner she has been accustomed to, but I can support her in the way her mother was accustomed to when she was first married."

☆　☆　☆

Son: "Dad, what is a weapon?"

Father: "Why, son, that's something you fight with."

Son: "Is mother your weapon?"

☆　☆　☆

A little boy never said a word for six years. One day his parents served him cocoa. From out of left field the kid says, "This cocoa's no good." His parents went around raving. They said to him, "Why did you wait so long to talk?" He said, "Up till now everything's been okay."

☆ ☆ ☆

Father: "Don't you think our son gets all his brains from me?"
Mother: "Probably. I still have all mine."

☆ ☆ ☆

Parents spend the first part of a child's life urging him to walk and talk, and the rest of his childhood making him sit down and keep quiet.

☆ ☆ ☆

A third grader went home and told her mother she was in love with a classmate and was going to marry him. "That's fine," said her mother, going along with the gag. "Does he have a job?"
The little girl replied, "Oh, yes. He erases the blackboard in our class."

☆ ☆ ☆

Bride: "I don't want to forget any insignificant details."
Mother: "Don't worry! I'll be sure he's there!"

☆ ☆ ☆

Summertime is when parents pack off their troubles to an old Indian Camp and smile, smile, smile!

☆ ☆ ☆

Visitor: "Does your baby brother talk yet?"
Freddy: "He doesn't have to. He gets everything he wants by yelling."

☆   ☆   ☆

My boy is fifteen . . . going on twelve!

☆   ☆   ☆

"You look pretty dirty, Susie."
"Thank you. I look pretty when I'm clean, too."

☆   ☆   ☆

Announcement: The lodge meeting will be postponed. The Supreme Exalted Invincible Unlimited Sixty-Ninth Degree Potentate's wife wouldn't let him come!

☆   ☆   ☆

A message for all parents: Is your teen-age son or daughter out for the evening? If so, take advantage of the opportunity. Pack your furniture, call a moving van, and don't leave a forwarding address.

☆   ☆   ☆

Nothing annoys a woman more than to have friends drop in unexpectedly and find the house looking as it usually does.

☆   ☆   ☆

Mother: "How could you be so rude to tell your sister she's stupid. Tell her you're sorry."
Boy: "Sis, I'm sorry you're stupid!"

☆   ☆   ☆

109

On his first visit to the zoo, a little boy stared at the caged stork for a long while. Then he turned to his father and exclaimed, "Gee, Dad, he doesn't recognize me."

☆　☆　☆

"Young man, there were two cookies in the pantry this morning. May I ask how it happens that there is only one now?"

"Must have been so dark I didn't see the other one."

☆　☆　☆

Boy: "Dad, I just got a part in the school play. I play the part of a man that's been married for twenty-five years."

Father: "That's a good start, son. Just keep right at it and one of these days you'll get a speaking part!"

☆　☆　☆

Boy: "Dad, Mom just backed the car out of the garage and ran over my bicycle."

Father: "Serves you right, son, for leaving it on the front lawn."

☆　☆　☆

A six-year-old ran up and down the supermarket aisles shouting frantically, "Marian, Marian."

Finally reunited with his mother, he was chided by her, "You shouldn't call me 'Marian.' I'm your mother, you know."

"I know," he replied, "but the store is full of mothers."

☆　☆　☆

Father: "Son, do you realize when Lincoln was your age he was already studying hard to be a lawyer?"

Son: "Right, Pop, and when he was your age, he was already President of the United States!"

☆　☆　☆

A man in a supermarket was pushing a cart which contained, among other things, a screaming baby. As the man proceeded along the aisles, he kept repeating softly, "Keep calm, George. Don't get excited, George. Don't yell, George."

A lady watched with admiration and then said, "You are certainly to be commended for your patience in trying to quiet little George."

"Lady," he declared, "I'm George!"

☆　☆　☆

I know a teen-age girl who has been trying to run away from home for a year but every time she gets to the front door the phone rings.

☆　☆　☆

Wife I: "Does your husband have ulcers?"
Wife II: "No, but he's a carrier!"

☆　☆　☆

LIGHTWEIGHTS

If it wasn't for her Adam's apple, she wouldn't have any shape at all.

☆　☆　☆

With those varicose veins, she could win first prize at a costume party by going as a road map.

☆　　☆　　☆

He's so thin his muscles look like flea bites on a piece of spaghetti.

☆　　☆　　☆

When her husband takes her to a restaurant, the headwaiter asks him to check his umbrella.

☆　　☆　　☆

She recently swallowed an olive and was rushed to a maternity hospital.

☆　　☆　　☆

The world's skinniest kid is the girl who was so thin that if she stood sideways, she was marked absent. If she took a nickel out of her pocket, it threw her off balance.

☆　　☆　　☆

She is so thin it takes two of her to make a shadow.

☆　　☆　　☆

She has to run around in the shower to get wet.

☆　　☆　　☆

He was so thin he had to wear skis in the bathtub to keep from going down the drain.

☆　　☆　　☆

She was so thin that when she turned sideways and stuck out her tongue she looked like a zipper.

☆ ☆ ☆

If she would ever get a run in her nylons, she would fall out.

☆ ☆ ☆

MARRIAGE

I just heard of a man who met his wife at a travel bureau. She was looking for a vacation and he was the last resort.

☆ ☆ ☆

The best way for a man to remember his wife's birthday is to forget it just once.

☆ ☆ ☆

Views expressed by husbands are not necessarily those of the management.

☆ ☆ ☆

A lot of husbands have an impediment in their speech. Every time they open their mouth the wife interrupts.

☆ ☆ ☆

In my house, I make all the major decisions and my wife makes the minor ones. For example, I decide such things as East-West trade, crime in the streets, welfare cheating, and increase in taxes. My wife decides the minor things such as which house to buy, what kind of car we drive, how much money to spend, how to raise the children, etc.

☆   ☆   ☆

Being a husband is like any other job. It helps a lot if you like the boss.

☆   ☆   ☆

You can always tell when a marriage is shaky. The partners don't even talk to each other during a television commercial.

☆   ☆   ☆

Marriage is like a midnight phone call. You get a ring and then you wake up.

☆   ☆   ☆

It has been proven that married life is healthy. Statistics show that single people die sooner than married folks. So, if you're looking for a long life and a slow death, get married!

☆   ☆   ☆

Marriage counselor to wife: "Maybe your problem is that you've been waking up grumpy in the morning."

"No, I always let him sleep."

☆   ☆   ☆

A newly-married couple were entertaining, and among the guests was a man whose conduct was rather boisterous. At dinner he held up on his fork a piece of meat and in a vein of intended humor asked: "Is this pig?"

"To which end of the fork do you refer?" asked a quiet-looking man at the other end of the table.

☆　☆　☆

The honeymoon is over when he no longer smiles gently as he scrapes the burnt toast.

☆　☆　☆

The cooing usually stops when the honeymoon is over, but the billing goes on forever.

☆　☆　☆

A married couple trying to live up to a snobbish life style went to a party. The conversation turned to Mozart, "Absolutely brilliant . . . lovely . . . oh, a fine fellow . . . a genius, Mozart."

The woman, wanting to join in the general conversation, remarked casually, "Ah, Mozart. You're so right. I love him. Only this morning I saw him getting on the No. 5 bus going to Coney Island."

There was a sudden hush and everyone looked at her. Her husband was shattered. He pulled her away. "We're leaving right now. Get your coat and come."

In the car as they drove home, he kept muttering to himself. Finally, his wife turned to him.

"You are angry about something."

"Oh, really? You noticed it?" he sneered. "My goodness! I've never been so embarrassed in my life! You saw Mozart take the No. 5 bus to Coney Island! You idiot! Don't you know the No. 5 bus doesn't go to Coney Island?"

☆　☆　☆

He was escorting his wife to a concert and they arrived late. "What are they playing?" he whispered to his neighbor.

"The Fifth Symphony," replied the man.

"Well, thank goodness," sighed the husband. "I've missed four of them anyway."

☆　☆　☆

A Kansas cyclone hit a farmhouse just before dawn one morning. It lifted the roof off, picked up the beds on which the farmer and his wife slept, and set them down gently in the next county.

The wife began to cry.

"Don't be scared, Mary," her husband said. "We're not hurt."

Mary continued to cry. "I'm not scared," she responded between sobs. "I'm happy 'cause this is the first time in fourteen years we've been out together."

☆　☆　☆

"Was your wife outspoken?"

"Not by anyone I know of."

☆　☆　☆

"Did your wife have much to say when you got home last night?"

"No, but that didn't keep her from talking for two hours."

☆　☆　☆

Wife: "Scientists claim that the average person speaks 10,000 words a day."

Husband: "Yes, dear, but remember, you are far above average."

☆　☆　☆

Wife: "This is rabbit stew we're having."
Husband: "Thought so. I just found a hair in mine."

☆　☆　☆

Whenever my wife needs money, she calls me handsome. She says, "Hand some over."

☆　☆　☆

There are only two ways to handle a woman and nobody knows either of them.

☆　☆　☆

She puts mud on her face before going to bed at night. I say, "Goodnight, Swamp."

☆　☆　☆

Some people ask the secret of our long marriage. We take time to go to a restaurant two times a week. A little candlelight, dinner, soft music, and a slow walk home. She goes Tuesdays; I go Fridays.

☆　☆　☆

And speaking about all these marriages of high school kids, one elderly gent of twenty swore he attended one wedding ceremony where the bridegroom wept for two hours. It seems the bride got a bigger piece of cake than he did.

☆　☆　☆

He: "I love you terribly."
She: "You certainly do."

☆　☆　☆

Despite the statistics, he denies that married men live longer than single men . . . it only seems longer.

☆ ☆ ☆

One thing I'll say for my wife, she's a very neat housekeeper. If I drop my socks on the floor, she picks them up. If I throw my clothes around, she hangs them up. I got up at 3 o'clock the other morning, went in the kitchen to get a glass of orange juice. I came back and found the bed made.

☆ ☆ ☆

A man and his wife were returning to their seats after a movie intermission. In a voice of concern, he asked a man at the end of a row, "Did I step on your toes on the way out?"

"You certainly did," responded the other angrily.

"All right," he said, turning to his wife. "This is our row."

☆ ☆ ☆

Wife: "Honey, I can't get the car started. I think it's flooded."

Husband: "Where is it?"

Wife: "In the swimming pool."

Husband: "It's flooded."

☆ ☆ ☆

Husband: "Where is yesterday's newspaper?"

Wife: "I wrapped the garbage in it."

Husband: "Oh, I wanted to see it."

Wife: "There wasn't much to see . . . just some orange peels and coffee grounds."

☆ ☆ ☆

Husband: "Janice, when I see you in that hat, I laugh."

Wife: "Good! I'll put it on when the bill comes in."

☆　　☆　　☆

"I wonder if my husband will love me when my hair is gray?"

"Why not? He's loved you through three shades already."

☆　　☆　　☆

She refuses to give him a divorce. She says, "I've suffered with the bum for fifteen years, and now I should make him happy?"

☆　　☆　　☆

She's an angel . . . always up in the air and harping on something.

☆　　☆　　☆

I have been married thirty-six years and I don't regret one day of it. The one unregrettable day was July 8, 1953.

☆　　☆　　☆

Wife: "I just got back from the beauty shop."
Husband: "What was the matter? Was it closed?"

☆　　☆　　☆

A young man came home from the office and found his bride sobbing convulsively. "I feel terrible," she told him. "I was pressing your suit and I burned a big hole right in the seat of your trousers."

"Forget it," consoled her husband. "Remember that I've got an extra pair of pants for that suit."

"Yes, and it's lucky you have," said the little woman, drying her eyes. "I used them to patch the hole."

☆ ☆ ☆

Talk about an exciting weekend! Yesterday my wife and I were standing in front of a wishing well and she fell in. I didn't realize those things worked!

☆ ☆ ☆

"Now, that looks like a happily married couple."

"Don't be too sure, my dear. They're probably saying the same thing about us."

☆ ☆ ☆

"How long have you two been married?" asked a friend.

"We've been happily married for seven years," answered the husband. "Seven out of sixteen isn't bad."

☆ ☆ ☆

She: "I had to marry you to find out how stupid you are."

He: "You should have known that the minute I asked you."

☆ ☆ ☆

Husband overheard at a party muttering to his wife, "What did I say to offend you, dear? It might come in useful again sometime."

☆ ☆ ☆

"Hello, Sam," exclaimed Jim, meeting a buddy for the first time since the war's end. "Did you marry that girl you used to go with or are you still doing your own cooking and ironing?"

"Yes," replied Sam.

☆   ☆   ☆

A couple, just married, got among their wedding presents two tickets to a very fine show, with the notation "Guess who" on the tickets. They went to the play. When they returned, all of their wedding presents were gone, and a note was left also, "Now you know!"

☆   ☆   ☆

A sorely pressed newlywed sought valiantly to console his little bride, who sprawled, dissolved in tears, on the chaise lounge. "Darling," he implored, "believe me. I never said you were a terrible cook. I merely pointed out that our garbage disposal has developed an ulcer."

☆   ☆   ☆

Wife: "You both arrived at that cab at the same time. Why did you let him have it? Why didn't you stand up for your rights?"

Husband: "He needed it more than I did. He was late to his Karate class."

☆   ☆   ☆

She: "Will you love me when I am old and wrinkled?"

He: "Yes, I do!"

☆   ☆   ☆

Wife: "When we were younger, you used to nibble on my ear."

(The husband starts to leave the room)

Wife: "Where are you going?"

Husband: "To get my teeth!"

☆　　☆　　☆

"But, my dear," protested the henpecked husband, "I've done nothing. You've been talking for an hour and a half and I haven't said a word."

"I know," the wife replied. "But you listen like a wise-guy."

☆　　☆　　☆

Wife: "Look at the old clothes I have to wear. If anyone came to visit, they would think I was the cook!"

Husband: "Well, they'd change their minds if they stayed for dinner!"

☆　　☆　　☆

Wife: "George! Come quickly! A wild tiger has just gone into mother's tent!"

Husband: "Well, he got himself into that mess; let him get out of it!"

☆　　☆　　☆

Wife: "Darling, you know that cake you asked me to bake for you? Well, the dog ate it."

Husband: "That's okay, dear; don't cry. I'll buy you another dog!"

☆　　☆　　☆

"My wife spent four hours in the beauty shop the other day."

"Boy, that's a long time."
"Yeah, and that was just for the estimate!"

☆　☆　☆

Wife: "I dreamed you gave me $100 for summer clothes last night. You wouldn't spoil that dream, would you, dear?"
Husband: "Of course not, darling. You may keep the $100."

☆　☆　☆

Did you hear about the man who asked the bellboy to carry his bag? The bellboy came over and picked up his wife.

☆　☆　☆

Husband: "That is a beautiful turkey for Thanksgiving! What kind of stuffing did you use?"
Wife: "This one wasn't hollow!"

☆　☆　☆

My husband really embarrassed me the other day in a restaurant. When he drank his soup, six couples got up and started to dance.

☆　☆　☆

Husband: "Do you think you can paint a good portrait of my wife?"
Artist: "My friend, I can make it so lifelike you'll jump every time you see it."

☆　☆　☆

Husband: "Where did you get that new hat?"
Wife: "Don't worry, dear. It didn't cost a thing. It

was marked down from $20 to $10. So, I bought it with the $10 I saved."

☆ ☆ ☆

Wife: "I think you only married me because my daddy left me a lot of money."

Husband: "That's not true. I didn't care who left you the money!"

☆ ☆ ☆

MEDICAL

Doctor: "Say, the check you gave me for my doctor bill came back."

Patient: "So did my arthritis!"

☆ ☆ ☆

"What are you taking for your cold?"

"I don't know. What will you give me?"

☆ ☆ ☆

Doctor: "Are you still taking the cough medicine I gave you?"

Patient: "No, I tasted it and decided I'd rather have the cough."

☆ ☆ ☆

His psychiatrist just told him, "You haven't got an inferiority complex. You are inferior."

☆ ☆ ☆

Patient: "Doctor, it's 2 a.m. and I can't sleep. It is the bill I owe you. I can't pay it. It bothers me so much I can't sleep."

Doctor: "Why did you have to tell me that? Now I can't sleep."

☆ ☆ ☆

Doctor: "I see you're coughing better this morning."

Patient: "Why not? I've been practicing all night."

☆ ☆ ☆

Two eminently successful psychoanalysts occupied offices in the same building. One was forty years old, the other over seventy. They rode on the elevator together at the end of an unbearably hot, sticky day. The younger man was completely done in, and he noted with some resentment that his senior was fresh as a daisy. "I don't understand," he marveled, "how you can listen to drooling patients from morning till night on a day like this and still look so spry and unbothered when it's over."

The older analyst said simply, "Who listens?"

☆ ☆ ☆

Talk about children mimicking their parents! I understand Hollywood kids don't play doctor and nurse anymore. It's psychiatrist and psychoneurotic!

☆ ☆ ☆

Mrs. Jones was taken suddenly ill in the night, and a new doctor was called. After a look at the patient, the doctor stepped outside the sickroom to ask Mr. Jones for a corkscrew. Given the tool, he disappeared but several minutes later was back demanding a pair of pliers. Again he disappeared into the room of the moaning patient, only to call out again, "A chisel and a mallet, quickly."

Mr. Jones could stand it no longer. "What is her trouble, doctor?"

"Don't know yet," was the reply. "Can't get my instrument bag open."

☆ ☆ ☆

A man pleaded with the psychiatrist, "You've got to help me. It's my son."

"What's the matter?"

"He's always eating mud pies. I get up in the morning and there he is in the backyard eating mud pies. I come home at lunch and he is eating mud pies. I come home at dinner and there he is in the backyard eating mud pies."

The psychiatrist reassured him, "Give the kid a chance. It's all a part of growing up. It'll pass."

"Well, I don't like it, and neither does his wife."

☆ ☆ ☆

Psychiatrist to patient: "You're quite right. A man *is* following you constantly. He's trying to collect the $200 you owe me."

☆ ☆ ☆

The latest thing in psychiatry is group therapy. Instead of couches, they use bunk beds.

☆ ☆ ☆

Patient: "Doctor, I have an awful pain every time I lift my arm."

Doctor: "So, don't lift it!"

☆ ☆ ☆

126

Two psychiatrists met on the street. One smiled brightly and said, "Good morning!" The other walked on and muttered to himself, "I wonder what he meant by that!"

☆ ☆ ☆

Dentist: "What kind of filling would you like in your tooth?"
Boy: "Chocolate!"

☆ ☆ ☆

George was having trouble with a toothache, so he decided to visit the dentist.
"What do you charge for extracting a tooth?" George asked.
"Five dollars," replied the dentist.
"Five dollars for only two minutes' work?" exclaimed George.
"Well," replied the dentist, "if you wish, I can extract it very slowly."

☆ ☆ ☆

Doctor: "I have some good news and some bad news. Which do you want first?"
Patient: "Give me the bad news first."
Doctor: "We amputated the wrong leg."
Patient: "What is the good news?"
Doctor: "Your other leg won't need to be amputated after all."

☆ ☆ ☆

Surgeons invited to dinner parties are often asked to carve the meat—or worse yet, to watch the host carve while commenting on the surgeon's occupation. At one party, a surgeon friend was watching the carving while his host kept up a running commentary: "How am I doing, doc? How do you like that technique? I'd make a pretty good surgeon, don't you think?"

When the host finished and the slices of meat lay neatly on the serving platter, the surgeon spoke up: "Anybody can take them apart, Harry. Now let's see you put them back together again."

☆ ☆ ☆

"I had an operation and the doctor left a sponge in me."

"Got any pain?"

"No, but, boy, do I ever get thirsty!"

☆ ☆ ☆

He always feels bad when he feels good for fear he'll feel worse when he feels better.

☆ ☆ ☆

Inscription on the tombstone of a hypochondriac: "Now will you believe I'm sick?"

☆ ☆ ☆

Patient: "My right foot hurts."

Doctor: "It's just old age."

Patient: "But my left foot is just as old. How come it doesn't hurt?"

☆ ☆ ☆

On his sixth call following a dangerous operation, the doctor was surprised to hear the patient say: "Doctor, I am feeling so much better. I want you to let me have your bill."

"Nonsense, my good man," replied the physician. "You are far from strong enough for that."

☆　　☆　　☆

He's so full of penicillin that every time he sneezes he cures a dozen people.

☆　　☆　　☆

He is such a hypochondriac he won't even talk on the phone to anyone who has a cold.

☆　　☆　　☆

He is a very fine doctor. If you can't afford the operation, he touches up the X-rays.

☆　　☆　　☆

He's so anemic he has to get a transfusion in order to bleed.

☆　　☆　　☆

Doctors keep telling us to get lots of fresh air, but they never tell us where to find it.

☆　　☆　　☆

Did you hear about the poor fellow who told his doctor he heard music every time he put his hat on? The doctor fixed him right up. He took the guy's hat and removed the band.

☆　　☆　　☆

Did you hear about the man who swallowed his glass eye and rushed to a stomach specialist? The specialist peered down the unfortunate fellow's throat and exclaimed, "I've looked into a lot of stomachs in my day, but I must say, this is the first one that ever looked back at me."

☆　☆　☆

Did you hear about the doctor who wrote out a prescription in the usual doctor's fashion? The patient used it for two years as a railroad pass. Twice it got him into Radio City Music Hall, and once into Yankee Stadium. It came in handy as a letter from his employer to the cashier to increase his salary. And to cap the climax, his daughter played it on the piano and won a scholarship to the Curtis Music Conservatory.

☆　☆　☆

Two women went to the movies and one of them started to cough. Her friend leaned away from her. The more she coughed, the farther her friend tried to move away. Finally, the cougher turned around to her friend and said, "Look, you don't have to move away like that. This is not a sickness." Her friend replied, "Well, it isn't a wellness."

☆　☆　☆

"Doctor, will I be able to read with these new glasses?"
"Yes, of course."
"Good! I never could read before."

☆　☆　☆

"I've been seeing spots in front of my eyes."
"Have you seen a doctor?"
"No, just spots."

☆　☆　☆

Looking down at the sick man, the doctor decided to tell him the truth. "I feel that I should tell you: you are a very sick man. I'm sure you would want to know the facts. I don't think you have much time left. Now, is there anyone you would like to see?"

Bending down toward his patient, the doctor heard him feebly answer, "Yes."

"Who is it?"

In a slightly stronger tone, the sufferer said, "Another doctor."

☆　☆　☆

I won't say he's neurotic, but last week he was watching the Army-Navy game on television and every time one of the teams went into a huddle he wondered if they were talking about him.

☆　☆　☆

Now they've got a tranquilizer atomizer . . . one spray and it calms you down to the point where you can take a pill.

☆　☆　☆

I went to my doctor last week and he told me to take a hot bath before retiring. But that's ridiculous! It'll be years before I retire!

☆　☆　☆

When I got the bill for my operation, I found out why they wear masks in the operating room.

☆　☆　☆

A violinist was advised by the surgeon that he'd have to undergo an operation.

"But, doctor," intoned the patient, "I have concerts booked ahead. If you operate, can I be assured that I'll be able to play the violin in two weeks' time?"

"Undoubtedly!" assured the doctor. "The last patient on whom I performed this operation was playing a harp within twenty-four hours!"

☆　☆　☆

A lady with a bad rash visited a dermatologist. It was the type of condition that had been present for some time.

"Have you been treated for this rash before?" inquired the doctor.

"Yes, by my druggist."

"And what sort of foolish advice did he give you?" asked the doctor.

"Oh, he told me to come to see you."

☆　☆　☆

My arm started to hurt me and I asked the doctor to examine it. He looked at my arm and brought out a medical book and studied it for fifteen minutes. He said to me, "Have you ever had that pain before?" I said, "Yes." He said, "Well, you got it again."

☆　☆　☆

Mr. Jones phoned the doctor for an appointment. The nurse said she could give him an appointment in two weeks.

"In two weeks I could be dead!" wailed Jones.

"Well, in that case," answered the nurse, "you can always cancel the appointment!"

☆　☆　☆

A doctor had a problem with a leak in his bathroom plumbing that became bigger and bigger. Even though it was 2 a.m., the doctor decided to phone his plumber.

"For Pete's sake, Doc," he wailed, "this is some time to wake a guy."

"Well," the doctor answered testily, "you've never hesitated to call me in the middle of the night with a medical problem. Now it just happens I've got a plumbing emergency."

There was a moment's silence. Then the plumber spoke up, "Right you are, Doc," he agreed. "Tell me what's wrong."

The doctor explained about the leak in the bathroom.

"Tell you what to do," the plumber offered. "Take two aspirins every four hours and drop them down the pipe. If the leak hasn't cleared up by morning, phone me at the office."

☆ ☆ ☆

No wonder the Russians are getting so confident. If they've been watching television, they must figure every American has either tired blood, indigestion, or nagging headaches.

☆ ☆ ☆

Sam: "Why do doctors and nurses wear masks?"
Pete: "So that if someone makes a mistake no one will know who did it."

☆ ☆ ☆

The doctor told me to take this medicine after a hot bath. I could hardly finish drinking the bath!

☆ ☆ ☆

MISCELLANEOUS

"I caught a 250 pound marlin the other day!"

"That's nothing. I was fishing and hooked a lamp from an old Spanish ship. In fact, the light was still lit!"

"If you will blow out the light, I'll take 200 pounds off the marlin!"

☆ ☆ ☆

A woman went to her psychiatrist and said, "Doctor, I want to talk to you about my husband. He thinks he's a refrigerator."

"That's not so bad," said the doctor. "It's rather a harmless complex."

"Well, maybe," replied the lady. "But he sleeps with his mouth open and the light keeps me awake."

☆ ☆ ☆

1st Man: "I think we should all confess our faults one to another. I've got a terrible habit of stealing!"

2nd Man: "I've got a terrible habit of lying!"

3rd Man: "I beat my wife!"

4th Man: "When no one is around, I get drunk!"

5th Man: "I've got the terrible habit of gossiping, and I can hardly wait to get out of here!"

☆ ☆ ☆

"We were so poor when I was a little boy I had to wear hand-me-down clothes!"

"So what? Everybody has to wear hand-me-downs!"

"But all I had were older sisters!"

☆ ☆ ☆

Man, (to woman on train) "That is the ugliest baby I have ever seen!"

Woman: "Conductor! Conductor! This man has just insulted my baby!"

Conductor: "Now, madam, don't get mad. I'll get a drink of water for you and a banana for your baby."

☆　☆　☆

"How do you know your family was poor?"

"Every time I passed someone in town, they would say, "There goes Joe. His poor family!"

☆　☆　☆

It is not always easy to say the right thing on the spur of the moment. We can sympathize with the chap who met an old friend after many years.

"How is your wife?"

"She is in heaven," replied the friend.

"Oh, I'm sorry," stammered the chap. Then he realized this was not the thing to say. "I mean," he stammered, "I'm glad." That seemed even worse so he blurted, "Well, what I really mean is, I'm surprised."

☆　☆　☆

Shoe salesman who had dragged out half his stock to a woman customer: "Mind if I rest a few minutes, lady? Your feet are killing me."

☆　☆　☆

Joe: "What are you doing with those two pillows under your arms?"

Moe: "These aren't pillows. They are five-year deodorant pads!"

☆　☆　☆

"Are you enjoying the bus ride?"

"Yes!"

"Then why are you riding with your eyes shut? Are you sick?"

"No, I'm okay. It's just that I hate to see women stand!"

☆　☆　☆

"Did you hear the story about the dirty window?"

"No."

"Well, that's okay. You couldn't see through it anyway!"

☆　☆　☆

"What did your husband get you for your birthday?"

"A smog device."

"Why a smog device."

"He said my breath was a major cause of air pollution."

☆　☆　☆

Newsboy: "Extra, extra! Read all about it—two men swindled."

Man: "Give me one. Say, there isn't anything about two men being swindled."

Newsboy: "Extra, extra! Three men swindled."

☆　☆　☆

"What are you doing?"

"I'm watering my beans."

"But there is no water coming out of the can."

"Do you see any beans?"

☆　☆　☆

"Say, mister, would you give me a quarter for a sandwich?"

"I dunno. Lemme see the sandwich!"

☆ ☆ ☆

"Did you take a bath today?"

"Why? Is one missing?"

☆ ☆ ☆

Lady: "I would like a pair of alligator shoes."

Man: "Yes, ma'am; what size is your alligator?"

☆ ☆ ☆

"You're the laziest man I ever saw. Don't you do anything quickly?"

"Yes, I get tired fast."

☆ ☆ ☆

"If you're such a good fortune-teller, you should be able to tell me the score of tonight's hockey game before it starts!"

"Before the game starts, the score will be nothing to nothing!"

☆ ☆ ☆

"I can't pay the rent this month."

"But you said that last month."

"I kept my word, didn't I?"

☆ ☆ ☆

An immigrant who worked his way up to the biggest fleet of pushcarts in the world knew he was dying and decided to face up to things. He, therefore, called an attorney to his bedside, and, after ordering his wife not to cry, started to dispose of his worldly possessions.

"My Cadillac with the push-button motorcycle cop detector I leave to my son, George."

"Better you should leave it to Joe," Bertha interrupted. "He's a better driver."

"So let it be Joe," he whispered. "My Rolls Royce with the specially constructed Ford hot-rod engine I bequeath to my daughter, Linda."

"You had better give it to your nephew, Willie," Bertha again interrupted. "He's a very conservative driver."

"All right, give it to Willie. My twelve-cylinder Volvo I give to my niece, Sally."

"Personally, I think Judy should get it."

Unable to take more, he raised his head from the pillow and shouted, "Bertha, please, who's dying? You or me?"

☆　　☆　　☆

"Have any big men ever been born in this town?"
"No, just little babies."

☆　　☆　　☆

"Mr. Editor, do you think I should put more fire into my stories?"
"No, just the opposite."

☆　　☆　　☆

A man was waiting at an intersection for a circus to pass by. He saw a sign on one of the wagons that read: "Barney's Circus with Fifty Elephants." He counted the elephants as they crossed the intersection. When he got to fifty, he put his car in gear and started to cross the intersection because he was late for an appointment. Unfortunately, he had miscounted and his car hit and killed the last elephant.

138

A week later he got a notice from the circus that he'd have to pay $200,000. He called the circus manager and inquired, "What's the deal? I only hit one lousy elephant! Why do you want $200,000?"

The manager responded, "It's true, you only hit one elephant but you pulled the tails out of forty-nine others!"

☆   ☆   ☆

Did you hear about the spinster who could not see too well? In order to hide her failing eyesight from her intended, she stuck a pin in a tree. The next day, while walking in the forest with him, she pointed to the tree, some hundred yards distant, and said, "Isn't that a pin sticking in that tree?" And as she ran to retrieve it, she tripped over a cow.

☆   ☆   ☆

Little Girl: "Grandfather, make like a frog."

Grandfather: "What do you mean, make like a frog?"

Little Girl: "Mommy says we're going to make a lot of money when you croak!"

☆   ☆   ☆

A man put a coin in a vending machine and watched helplessly while the cup failed to appear. One nozzle sent coffee down the drain while another poured cream after it.

"Now that's real automation!" he exclaimed. "It even drinks for you!"

☆   ☆   ☆

Two men were digging a ditch on a very hot day. One said to the other, "Why are we down in this hole digging a ditch when our boss is standing up there under the shade of a tree?" "I don't know," responded the other. "I'll ask him."

So he climbed out of the hole and went to his boss. "Why are we digging in the hot sun and you are standing in the shade?" "Intelligence," the boss said. "What do you mean, 'intelligence?' " The boss said, "Well, I'll show you. I'll put my hand on this tree and I want you to hit it with your fist as hard as you can." The ditch digger took a mighty swing and tried to hit the boss' hand. The boss removed his hand and the ditch digger hit the tree. The boss said, "That's intelligence!"

The ditch digger went back to his hole. His friend asked, "What did he say?" "He said we are down here because of intelligence." "What's intelligence?" said the friend. The ditch digger put his hand on his face and said, "Take your shovel and hit my hand."

☆　　☆　　☆

The inmates of a prison had a joke book they all had memorized. The way they recited them was by the number of the joke. Some fellow would call out a number from one to one hundred and all would laugh.

A new man in the prison, after studying the book, said he wanted to tell a joke. They said, "O.K., shoot!"

He said, "Number 20," but nobody laughed. He said, "This is funny. What's wrong; why aren't you laughing?"

A fellow nearby said, "Some can tell them and some can't."

☆　　☆　　☆

A village blacksmith working at his open forge, hammering a white-hot horseshoe, had just finished the shoe and thrown it to the ground to cool.

The local wise-guy walked in at that moment. He picked up the horseshoe, but dropped it with a howl of pain.

"Pretty hot, eh?" asked the blacksmith.

"Naw," said the wise-guy. "It just don't take me long to look over a horseshoe."

☆　　☆　　☆

An old miser, because of his exceptional thrift, had no friends. Just before he died he called his doctor, lawyer, and minister together around his bedside. "I have always heard you can't take it with you, but I am going to prove you can," he said. "I have $90,000 in cash under my mattress. It's in three envelopes of $30,000 each. I want each of you to take one envelope now and just before they throw the dirt on me you throw the envelopes in."

The three attended the funeral and each threw his envelope into the grave. On the way back from the cemetery, the minister said, "I don't feel exactly right. I'm going to confess. I needed $10,000 badly for a new church we are building, so I took out $10,000 and threw only $20,000 in the grave."

The doctor said, "I, too, must confess. I am building a hospital and took $20,000 and threw in only $10,000."

The lawyer said, "Gentlemen, I'm surprised, shocked, and ashamed of you. I don't see how you could hold out that money. I threw in my personal check for the full amount."

☆　　☆　　☆

A hunter shot a duck and it fell into the lake. Quickly, he commanded his dog—a dog he had never worked before—to retrieve. The hound ran to the edge of the water, sniffed and walked out onto the waters of the lake. The hunter was amazed. He shot another duck; it, too, fell into the lake. Again the hound walked out on the water to retrieve the duck before it sank. At last, the hunter thought, he had something to show that friend of his who never let anything get to him. The next day the hunter suggested to his friend that they go do a little duck shooting. His friend shot a duck, and it fell into the lake. The dog walked across the water to retrieve it and drop it at the shooter's feet.

The hunter asked his friend, "What do you think of my bird dog? Didn't you notice anything special about my dog?"

"I noticed one thing. He can't swim."

☆　　☆　　☆

Fortunate was the Wilmington lady who lost her handbag in a shopping center—an honest lad found it and returned it to her. "Funny," commented the lady, "when I misplaced the bag there was a ten dollar bill in it. Now I find ten one dollar bills."

"That's right, lady," agreed the honest lad. "The last time I found a lady's purse, she didn't have any change for a reward."

☆　　☆　　☆

I now have 180 books but I have no bookcase—nobody will lend me a bookcase.

☆　　☆　　☆

"I'm not a liar, sir. I just remember big!"

☆　　☆　　☆

If the garbage workers in your community ever go out on strike, you might like to know how a wise New Yorker disposed of his refuse for the nine days the sanitation workers were off the job last summer. Each day he wrapped his garbage in gift paper. Then he put it in a shopping bag. When he parked his car, he left the bag on the front seat with the window open. When he got back to the car, the garbage always had been collected.

☆   ☆   ☆

Most of us have two chances of becoming wealthy . . . slim and none.

☆   ☆   ☆

I saw a hippie running after a garbage truck this morning, yelling, "Taxi! Taxi!"

☆   ☆   ☆

When some people retire, nobody knows the difference.

☆   ☆   ☆

A man seldom makes the same mistake twice. Generally, it's three times or more.

☆   ☆   ☆

Next time you start to believe you are indispensable, stick your finger in a bowl of water. Now remove it. See the impression you've made?

☆   ☆   ☆

"Oh! Oh! I'm hit!"
"You shot bad, Tex?"
"You ever hear of anyone being shot good?"

☆   ☆   ☆

Joe and Bill met on a street corner. When Joe said he sure was glad to see his friend, Bill answered, "How can you see me when I'm not even here? And I'll bet you $10 I can prove it!"

"You're going to bet me $10 you're not here? Okay, it's a bet. Go ahead and prove it."

"Am I in Chicago?"

"Nope."

"Am I in New York?"

Joe answered emphatically, "No!"

"Well, if I'm not in Chicago and I'm not in New York, that means I'm in some other place, right?"

"That's right."

"Well, if I'm in some other place, I can't be here. I'll take that $10."

"How can I give you the money if you're not here?"

☆   ☆   ☆

A man dropped in to pay a friend an unexpected visit, and was amazed to find him playing chess with a dog. The man watched in silence for a few minutes, then burst out with, "That's the most incredible dog I ever saw in my life!" "Oh, he isn't so smart," was the answer. "I've beaten him three games out of four."

☆   ☆   ☆

An elderly widower loved his cat so dearly he tried to teach it to talk. "If I can get Tabby to converse with me," he reasoned, "I won't have to bother with ornery humans at all." First, he tried a diet of canned salmon, then one of canaries. Tabby obviously approved of both but he didn't learn to talk. Then one day the widower had two parrots cooked in butter and served to Tabby with asparagus and French-fried potatoes. Tabby licked the plate clean, and then . . . wonder of wonders . . . suddenly turned to her master and shouted, "Look out!"

Possibly the widower didn't hear because he never moved a muscle. The next moment the ceiling caved in and buried him under a mass of debris. The cat shook its head and said in disgust, "Eight years he spends getting me to talk and then the idiot doesn't listen."

☆　　☆　　☆

In front of a delicatessen, an art connoisseur noticed a mangy little kitten, lapping up milk from a saucer. The saucer, he realized with a start, was a rare and precious piece of pottery.

He sauntered into the store and offered two dollars for the cat. "It's not for sale," said the proprietor. "Look," said the collector, "that cat is dirty and undesirable, but I'm eccentric. I like cats that way. I'll raise my offer to five dollars." "It's a deal," said the proprietor, and pocketed the five spot.

"For that sum I'm sure you won't mind throwing in the saucer," said the connoisseur. "The kitten seems so happy drinking from it."

"Nothing doing," said the proprietor firmly. "That's my lucky saucer. From that saucer so far this week, I've sold thirty-four cats."

☆　　☆　　☆

Creditors have better memories than debtors.

☆　　☆　　☆

A big hulk of a man, somewhat sinister in appearance, accosted a small, dapper gentleman on the street, and asked, "C-c-can you t-t-tell m-m-me how to g-g-get to C-C-City Hall?"

The small man paled and, turning on his heels fled down the street. Angered and exasperated, the big man pursued him. They raced for several blocks until the little man's wind gave out and he was overtaken and captured. The big man seized him by the arm and cried angrily, "W-w-what do you m-m-mean . . . running away w-w-when I ask y-y-you a c-c-civil question?"

The little man looked up and gasped, "D-d-do you t-t-think I w-w-wanted m-m-my block k-k-knocked off?"

☆ ☆ ☆

"I haven't slept for days."
"How come?"
"I only sleep at night."

☆ ☆ ☆

A boastful Britisher was holding forth on the merits of his watch to friends in New York City. At last one of the Americans decided he could stand it no longer.

"That's nothing," he interrupted. "I dropped my watch into the Hudson a year ago, and it's been running ever since."

The Englishman looked taken aback.

"What?" he exclaimed. "The same watch?"

"No," he replied, "the Hudson."

☆ ☆ ☆

One out of four Americans is mentally ill. Next time you're in a group of four people, take a good look at the other three. If they look all right, you're it!

☆ ☆ ☆

A farmer had a wife who was very critical of his grammar. One evening he told her he had a friend named Bill he would like for her to meet.

"Don't call him 'Bill,' " she insisted. "Call him 'William.' "

When the friend arrived, the farmer said, "Let me tell you a tale."

"Not tale," the wife interrupted. "Say, 'anecdote.' "

That night, upon retiring, the farmer told her to put out the light.

"Not 'put out,' " she exclaimed. "Say, 'extinguish' the light."

Later in the night she awakened her husband and sent him downstairs to investigate a noise. When he returned, she asked him what it was.

"It was," he explained carefully, "a William goat which I took by its anecdote and extinguished."

☆　☆　☆

"Once a friend of mine and I agreed it would be helpful for each of us to tell the other all our faults."

"How did it work?"

"We haven't spoken for five years."

☆　☆　☆

"Those are fighting words where I come from!"

"Well, why don't you fight then?"

"'Cause I ain't where I come from."

☆　☆　☆

"What a lot of friends we lose through their borrowing money from us."

"Yes, it is touch and go with most of them."

☆　☆　☆

A Texan was visiting Scotland and every time his host would show him a sight he would say, "That's nothing! We've got the same thing in Texas, only better!"

Finally they arrived at Loch Lomond. The Texan said, "Well, you have one thing that we don't have in Texas. This is a pretty lake."

The host said, "Well, you could dig a pipeline from Texas under the ocean and into the lake. And if you can suck as hard as you can blow, the lake is yours."

☆ ☆ ☆

Since he lost his money, half his friends don't know him anymore. And the other half? They don't know yet he has lost it.

☆ ☆ ☆

"Thankful! What have I to be thankful for? I can't pay any of my bills!"

"Then, be thankful you aren't one of the creditors."

☆ ☆ ☆

Mrs. Brown must be offended at something. She hasn't been over for several days. Be sure to find out what it is when she does come over, and we'll try it on her again.

☆ ☆ ☆

Lady: "Oh, isn't he sweet. . . . Little boy, if you give me a kiss, I'll give you a bright new penny."

Little Boy: "I get twice as much at home for just taking castor oil."

☆ ☆ ☆

FAMOUS LAST WORDS:

"You can make it easy—that train isn't coming fast."

"Gimme a match. I think my gas tank is empty."

"Wife, these biscuits are tough."

"Let's see if it's loaded."

"Step on her, boy, we're only going seventy-five."

"Just watch me dive from that bridge."

"If you knew anything you wouldn't be a traffic cop."

"Lemme have that bottle; I'll try it."

"What? Your mother is going to stay another month?"

"Say, who's boss of this joint, anyhow?"

☆　　☆　　☆

Mark Twain once encountered a friend at the races who said, "I'm broke. I wish you'd buy me a ticket back to town."

Twain said, "Well, I'm pretty broke myself but I'll tell you what to do. You hide under my seat and I'll cover you with my legs." It was agreed and Twain then went to the ticket office and bought two tickets. When the train was underway and the supposed stowaway was snug under the seat, the conductor came by and Twain gave him the two tickets.

"Where is the other passenger?" asked the conductor.

Twain tapped on his forehead and said in a loud voice, "That is my friend's ticket. He is a little eccentric and likes to ride under the seat."

☆　　☆　　☆

Three polar bears were sitting on an iceberg. All were cold and quiet. Finally, the father bear said, "Now I've a tale to tell."

"I, too, have a tale to tell," said the mother bear.

The little polar bear looked up at his parents and said, "My tale is told!"

☆　　☆　　☆

My hotel room was so small the mice were hunch-backed.

☆　　☆　　☆

Judy: "What did you do to your hair? It looks like a wig."

Joan: "It is a wig."

Judy: "You know? You could never tell!"

☆　　☆　　☆

A couple in Hollywood got divorced. Then they got remarried. The divorce didn't work out.

☆　　☆　　☆

A man I know solved the problem of too many visiting relatives. He borrowed money from the rich ones and loaned it to the poor ones. Now none of them come back.

☆　　☆　　☆

A gorilla walked into a drugstore and ordered a fifty-cent sundae. He put down a ten dollar bill to pay for it. The clerk thought, "What can a gorilla know about money?" So he handed back a single dollar in change.

As he did, he said, "You know, we don't get many gorillas in here."

150

"No wonder," answered the gorilla, "at nine dollars a sundae."

☆　　☆　　☆

A newsman sent a letter home from Red China. At the end he put a note, "I hope this letter reaches you. The censors are very tough." When the letter arrived, another note had been added, "There are no censors in the People's Republic of China."

☆　　☆　　☆

Last night I dreamed I ate a five-pound marshmallow. When I woke up, my pillow was gone.

☆　　☆　　☆

Betty: "I wish I had enough money to buy an elephant."
Joe: "Why do you want an elephant?"
Betty: "I don't. I just want the money."

☆　　☆　　☆

Now for a couple of dillies: DILLY, DILLY.

☆　　☆　　☆

Blow: "Did you hear the smartest kid in the world is becoming deaf?"
Joe: "No, tell me about it."
Blow: "What did you say?"

☆　　☆　　☆

A man tried to sell his neighbor a new dog.
"This is a talking dog," he said. "And you can have him for five dollars."
The neighbor said, "Who do you think you're

kidding with this talking dog stuff? There ain't no such animal."

Suddenly the dog looked up with tears in his eyes. "Please buy me, sir," he pleaded. "This man is cruel. He never buys me a meal, never bathes me, never takes me for a walk. And I used to be the richest trick dog in America. I performed before kings. I was in the Army and was decorated ten times."

"Hey!" said the neighbor. "He can talk. Why do you want to sell him for just five dollars?"

"Because," said the seller, "I'm getting tired of all his lies."

☆　☆　☆

A fellow had been standing in line to get into a movie theater. He was surprised when he reached the box office because the price for the ticket was $2.50. He pointed to a sign that said "popular prices" and said, "You call $2.50 'popular'?"

"We like it," answered the girl sweetly.

☆　☆　☆

Two men were riding on a train for the first time. They brought bananas for lunch. Just as one of them bit into his banana, the train entered a tunnel.

First Man: "Did you take a bite of your banana?"
Second Man: "No."
First Man: "Well, don't! I did and went blind!"

☆　☆　☆

Sue: "See that woman over there? She's been married four times—once to a millionaire; then to an actor; third, to a minister; and last to an undertaker."

Sal: "I know! One for the money, two for the show, three to get ready and four to go."

☆　☆　☆

152

And then there are people who claim movies would be better if they shot less films and more actors.

☆   ☆   ☆

Here it is the middle of January and we're still cleaning up from Christmas. Last week we cleaned out our checking account; this week we cleaned out our savings account.

☆   ☆   ☆

So this Italian immigrant walks into a Fifth Avenue bank and says, "Pardon mia, I'd like to talk with the fella what arranges loans." The guard replies, "I'm sorry but the loan arranger is out to lunch." "In data case, I talk to Tonto!"

☆   ☆   ☆

I used to box. My best punch was a rabbit punch, but they would never let me fight rabbits.

☆   ☆   ☆

Joe: "Is that all there is to the story?"
Joan: "I guess so. I've already told you more than I heard."

☆   ☆   ☆

Did you hear about the undertaker who closes all his letters with: "Eventually yours"?

☆   ☆   ☆

A little boy came home from school crying, "Mommy, Mommy. The kids at school called me a three-headed monster."

The mother responded sympathetically: "Now, there, there, there."

☆   ☆   ☆

I have discovered an easy way to get rich. You buy fifty female pigs and fifty male deer and put them together. Then you will have one hundred sows and bucks.

☆   ☆   ☆

I hear they're putting up a $20,000,000 hotel right in the heart of Moscow. Gonna call it the "Comrade Hilton."

☆   ☆   ☆

Remember the good old days when the still, small voice within us used to be called conscience instead of a transistor radio?

☆   ☆   ☆

I understand the only people in the world who have no juvenile delinquency problem are the Eskimos . . . and it's all because of whale blubber. The minute a kid steps out of line they whale him till he blubbers!

☆   ☆   ☆

First Cowboy: "Why are you wearing only one spur?"
Second Cowboy: "Well, I figure when one side of the horse starts running, the other wide will too."

☆   ☆   ☆

Two kangaroos were talking to each other and one

said, "I hope it doesn't rain today. I just hate it when the children play inside."

☆ ☆ ☆

I love Christmas. I receive a lot of presents I just can't wait to exchange.

☆ ☆ ☆

One time when my friend was in the breeding business, he crossed a parrot with a tiger. He doesn't know what it is, but when it talks everybody listens!

☆ ☆ ☆

Terry: "Say something soft and sweet."
Jerry: "Marshmallow."

☆ ☆ ☆

Stu: "I guess my pen will just have to go on itching."
Sue: "Why?"
Stu: "I'm all out of scratch paper."

☆ ☆ ☆

The only thing that keeps my house from falling down is that the termites are holding hands.

☆ ☆ ☆

"Knock, knock."
"Who's there?"
"Honeydew and cantaloupe."
"Honeydew and cantaloupe who?"
"Honeydew you love me? We cantaloupe now."

☆ ☆ ☆

"Knock, knock."
"Who's there?"
"Oswald."
"Oswald who?"
"Oswald mah gum."

☆　☆　☆

"Knock, knock."
"Who's there?"
"Divan."
"Divan who?"
"Divan the bathtub—I'm dwoning."

☆　☆　☆

A Vic Tanny graduate was boasting about his strength and went on about it for some time. A gardener overheard and made him this offer, "Tell you what, I'll bet you $25 I can wheel a load in this wheelbarrow over there to the other side of the street that you can't wheel back."

"You're on," said Mr. Motormouth. "What's your load going to be?"

"Get in," said the gardener.

☆　☆　☆

Joe: "Woman the lifeboats! Woman the lifeboats!"
Moe: "You don't 'woman' the lifeboats. That's silly. You 'man' the lifeboats!"
Joe: "You fill your lifeboats and I'll fill mine."

☆　☆　☆

City Slicker: "Look at that bunch of cows."
Farmer: "Not bunch .... herd."
City Slicker: "Heard what?"
Farmer: "Herd of cows."

City Slicker: "Sure I've heard of cows."

Farmer: "No, a cow herd."

City Slicker: "Why should I care what a cow heard? I've got no secrets from a cow."

☆ ☆ ☆

Joe: "What kind of dog is that?"

Blow: "He's a police dog."

Joe: "He sure doesn't look like one to me."

Blow: "Of course not. He's in the secret service."

☆ ☆ ☆

A guide was showing a Texan Niagara Falls.

Guide: "I'll bet you don't have anything like that in Texas."

Texan: "Nope, I reckon we don't; but we got plumbers that could fix it."

☆ ☆ ☆

Larry: "You told me if I rubbed grease on my chest I'd grow tall like you, but it didn't work."

Harry: "What did you use?"

Larry: "Crisco."

Harry: "Stupid; that's shortening."

☆ ☆ ☆

A man who was late in paying his bills received the following note: "Your account has been on our books for over a year. Just want to remind you we have now carried you longer than your mother did."

☆ ☆ ☆

"Did you hear about the guy that had three wives in three months? The first two died of poisoned mushrooms."

"What happened to the third wife?"

"She died from a blow on the head. She wouldn't eat the mushrooms!"

☆　　☆　　☆

"I've invented a computer that's almost human."

"You mean, it can think?"

"No. But when it makes a mistake it can put the blame on another computer."

☆　　☆　　☆

A man from the deep South was about to jump from the window of a building when a passerby saw him and tried to talk him out of it. "For the sake of your mother, don't do it!" the passerby pleaded.

"I don't have a mother."

"Well, think of your father."

"I don't have a father."

"Well, think of your wife."

"I never married."

"Well, then, think of Robert E. Lee!"

"Robert E. Lee? Who's he?"

"Never mind, Yankee. Go ahead and jump!"

☆　　☆　　☆

First Reporter: "What shall I say about the peroxide blondes who made such a fuss at the ball game?"

Second Reporter: "Just say the bleachers went wild."

☆　　☆　　☆

"You shouldn't worry like that. It doesn't do any good."

"It does for me! Ninety percent of the things I worry about never happen!"

☆　　☆　　☆

"This house," said the real estate salesman, "has both its good points and its bad points. To show you I'm honest, I'm going to tell you about both. The disadvantages are, that there is a chemical plant one block south and a slaughterhouse a block north."

"What are the advantages?" inquired the prospective buyer.

"The advantage is that you can always tell which way the wind is blowing."

☆　　☆　　☆

Hippie I: "There is only one thing that bugs me about this revolution bit."

Hippie II: "And what's that?"

Hippie I: "What happens to our unemployment checks when we overthrow the government?"

☆　　☆　　☆

Joe: "When I would wear my hand-me-downs to school, all the boys would make fun of me."

Moe: "What did you do?"

Joe: "I hit them over the head with my purse!"

☆　　☆　　☆

"Did you hear about the cross-eyed discus thrower?"

"No, did he set lots of records?"

"No, but he sure kept the crowd alert!"

☆　　☆　　☆

Did you hear about the farmer that decided to buy a chain saw? A logging foreman sold him one that he guaranteed would cut down fifteen trees in a single day. A week later, a very unhappy farmer came back to report that the power saw must be faulty—it averaged only three trees a day. The foreman grabbed the saw, pulled the cord, and the saw promptly went, "Bzzzzzzzzzzz."

"Hey," demanded the startled farmer, "what's that noise?"

☆ ☆ ☆

Sign on wishing well: WISH CAREFULLY. NO REFUNDS.

☆ ☆ ☆

Mike: "I always do my hardest work before breakfast."
Sandy: "What's that?"
Mike: "Getting up."

☆ ☆ ☆

Did you hear about the new invention? A square bathtub! It eliminates the ring!

☆ ☆ ☆

"It took me all morning to fill this salt shaker."
"Why all morning?"
"It's *hard* to get the salt through those little holes on the top!"

☆ ☆ ☆

The smog was so bad in Los Angeles that I felt the sights and went back home!

☆ ☆ ☆

As they left the auditorium after a two-hour lecture on 19th-century English poets, the wife exclaimed, "Didn't it make your mind soar?"

"Yes," her husband agreed grimly, "and my back-side, too!"

☆　☆　☆

A newspaper once carried an editorial which stated bluntly that half the city council were crooks. Under penalty of arrest, the editor issued the following retraction: "Half the city council aren't crooks."

☆　☆　☆

You can fool some of the people all of the time and all of the people some of the time, but most of the time they will make fools of themselves.

☆　☆　☆

Did you read where Liberace had a sequinned dinner jacket made up that cost him $3,000? Isn't that ridiculous? Anyone who pays more than $2,000 for a dinner jacket is plain crazy!

☆　☆　☆

Red: "Did you mark that place where the fishing was good?"

Ted: "Yes, I put an X on the side of the boat."

Red: "That was stupid. What if we should take out another boat next time?"

☆　☆　☆

A long-haired boy was trying to get into a swim club but was stopped by the owner who tried to explain that for health reasons long-haired boys were prohibited from using the pool.

"Get a haircut and you're welcome," said the owner.

"Some of history's greatest men had long hair," said the young man.

"Those are the rules."

"Moses had long hair."

"Moses can't swim in our pool, either."

☆　☆　☆

There were three men in a boat halfway across a lake. The first man suddenly said, "I forgot my lunch," got out of the boat and walked to shore on top of the water. Later, the second man said, "I forgot my fishing tackle," and also walked across the water to shore. By this time, the third man thought to himself, "They're not going to outsmart me. I forgot my bait can," and he started to walk across the water, but he sank. The first man said to the second, "Maybe we should have told him where the rocks were."

☆　☆　☆

ON THE ROAD

Sign on the Los Angeles boundary line: "You have just left the City of Los Angeles. Resume natural breathing."

☆　☆　☆

A motorist is a person who, after seeing a wreck, drives carefully for several blocks.

☆　☆　☆

Bud: "All this talk about backseat driving is hogwash. I've driven for fifteen years and I've never heard a word from back there."

Dud: "What kind of car do you drive?"

Bud: "A hearse."

☆   ☆   ☆

A lady driving along hit a guy. She yelled, "Watch out!"

He said, "Why? Are you coming back?"

☆   ☆   ☆

Nothing confuses a man more than driving behind a woman who does everything right!

☆   ☆   ☆

Those little cars have all kinds of advantages. Just this morning a motorcycle cop was chasing my Volkswagen. I knew I couldn't outrun him so I did the next best thing—drove up on the sidewalk and got lost in a crowd!

☆   ☆   ☆

I just solved the parking problem. I bought a parked car.

☆   ☆   ☆

Did you hear about the man who bought one of those British cars? He kept careful records for a month because everybody said the mileage was so sensational. Obviously, he wasn't getting what he was supposed to be getting. So he took the car to the mechanic and told him to check it out. The car was in perfect condition. The owner protested, "Look, I love this car, but evidently I am not getting the mileage that I am supposed to be getting." The mechanic looked at him and said, "Why don't you do what all other foreign car owners do?" "What's that?" "Lie about it."

☆　　☆　　☆

There was a hitchhiker walking down the road. A young man passed by in a sports car and asked, "Do you want to drag?"

So the hitchhiker started running and the young man speeded up to sixty miles an hour, looked back and saw the hitchhiker. The driver speeded up to 100 m.p.h. and the hitchhiker was still running behind him. Then the driver speeded up to 120 m.p.h. and the hitchhiker disappeared from sight.

The driver decided to turn back and find the hitchhiker to see what happened. There was the hitchhiker lying exhausted in a ditch.

"What happened?" asked the driver.

"You'd blow out a tennis shoe, too, if you were going 120 m.p.h.," said the hitchhiker.

☆　　☆　　☆

An insurance claim agent was teaching his wife to drive when the brakes suddenly failed on a steep, downhill grade.

"I can't stop!" she shrilled. "What should I do?"

"Brace yourself," advised her husband, "and try to hit something cheap."

☆　　☆　　☆

Angry customer: "I thought you said this was a good car. It won't even go uphill."

Used car dealer: "I said, 'On the level, it's a fine car.' "

☆　　☆　　☆

A motorist had a flat tire in front of the insane asylum. He took the wheel off, and the bolts that held the wheel on rolled down into the sewer.

An inmate, looking through the fence, suggested that the man take one bolt from the remaining three wheels to hold the fourth wheel in place until he could get to a service station.

The motorist thanked him profusely and said, "I don't know why you are in that place."

The inmate said, "I'm here for being crazy, not for being stupid."

☆　　☆　　☆

"I have a friend who is a real inventor. He took the fender from a Chevy, a motor from a Ford, and the transmission from a Sting Ray."

"Well, what did he get?"

"Three years."

☆　　☆　　☆

Did you hear about the cheerful truck driver who pulled up at a roadside cafe in the middle of the night for a dinner stop? Halfway through his dinner, three wild-looking motorcyclists roared up . . . bearded, leather-jacketed, filthy . . . with swastikas adorning their chests and helmets.

For no reason at all they selected the truck driver as a target. One poured pepper over his head, another stole his apple pie, the third deliberately upset his cup of coffee. The truck driver never said one word—just arose, paid his check, and exited.

"That trucker sure ain't much of a fighter," sneered one of the invaders. The girl behind the counter, peering out into the night, added, "He doesn't seem to be much of a driver either. He just ran his truck right over three motorcycles!"

☆　　☆　　☆

PICK ON SOMEONE ELSE!

Q: "Why doesn't General Motors give their Smogarian mechanics a coffee break?"
A: "Takes too long to retrain them."

☆　☆　☆

Q: "How many Smogarians does it take to change a light bulb?"
A: "Three. One to hold the bulb and two to turn the ladder."

☆　☆　☆

"Do you speak Smogarian?"
"No."
"Do you read Smogarian?"
"No."
"Do you write Smogarian?"
"No."
"Do you know how many Smogarians are in Smogaria?"
"No."
"How does it feel to be dumber than a Smogarian?"

☆　☆　☆

A perfect gift for a Smogarian who has everything . . . a garbage truck to keep it in.

☆　☆　☆

Did you know Smogarian dogs have flat noses? . . . from chasing parked cars.

☆　☆　☆

Did you hear about the Smogarian race track driver at Indianapolis who came in last? His average speed was 6.49 m.p.h. He had to make 75 pit stops—three for fuel, two to have the tires changed, and 70 to ask for directions.

☆　　☆　　☆

The most dangerous job in Smogaria . . . riding shotgun on a garbage truck.

☆　　☆　　☆

Q: "What's the capital of Smogaria?"
A: "About thirteen dollars."

☆　　☆　　☆

Did you hear about the Smogarian beauty contest? Nobody won.

☆　　☆　　☆

Q: "What's the difference between a Smogarian grandmother and an elephant?"
A: "About seven pounds."

☆　　☆　　☆

Dope ring? . . . that's twelve Smogarians sitting in a circle.

☆　　☆　　☆

Q: "Why don't Smogarians kill flies?"
A: "It is their national bird."

☆　　☆　　☆

"Did you hear about the Smogarian orchestra that

stopped in the middle of a performance to clean the saliva out of their instruments?''

"What's wrong with that?"

"This was a string orchestra."

☆   ☆   ☆

Q: "Do you know why it takes a Smogarian five days to wash his basement windows?"

A: "He needs four and a half days to dig the holes for the ladder."

☆   ☆   ☆

TEASERS

Q: "How do you avoid falling hair?"

A: "Jump out of the way."

☆   ☆   ☆

Q: "You load 16 tons and what do you get?"

A: "A hernia!"

☆   ☆   ☆

Q: "Name six animals that inhabit the Arctic region."

A: "Three seals and three polar bears."

☆   ☆   ☆

Q: "Which month has twenty-eight days?"

A: "They all have."

☆   ☆   ☆

Q: "Do you know what happened when they crossed an abalone with a crocodile?"
A: "A crock-a-baloney!"

☆　　☆　　☆

Q: "Do you know what they got when they crossed a gorilla with a porcupine?"
A: "I don't know what you call it but it sure gets a seat on the subway!"

☆　　☆　　☆

Q: "Do you know what they got when they crossed a rattlesnake with a horse?"
A: "'I don't know what you call it, but if it bites you you can ride it to the hospital!"

☆　　☆　　☆

Q: "What is the name of that lady with the wooden leg?"
A: "Peg!"

☆　　☆　　☆

Q: "What is practical nursing?"
A: "Falling in love with a rich patient!"

☆　　☆　　☆

Q: "What do they call a German hippie?"
A: "A flowerkraut!"

☆　　☆　　☆

Q: "Who invented the pendulum?"
A: "Pendulum Franklin."

☆　　☆　　☆

Q: "What weighs 2,500 pounds and wears flowers in its hair?"
A: "A hippiepotamus."

☆ ☆ ☆

Q: "What do they call a man who steals ham?"
A: "A hamburglar."

☆ ☆ ☆

Q: "Who was Alexander Graham Bell Pulaski?"
A: "The first telephone Pole."

☆ ☆ ☆

Q: "What's the best way to drive a baby buggy?"
A: "Tickle its feet."

☆ ☆ ☆

Q: "What would you get if you crossed a cow with a porcupine?"
A: "A steak with a built-in toothpick."

☆ ☆ ☆

Q: "If a rooster laid an egg on the top of a hill, which side would the egg roll down?"
A: "Neither side . . . a rooster can't lay eggs."

☆ ☆ ☆

Q: "Why does Santa Claus have three gardens?"
A: "So he can ho, ho, ho."

☆ ☆ ☆

Q: "What animal can jump higher than a house?"
A: "Any animal . . . a house can't jump!"

Q: "What did the boy octopus say to the girl octopus?"

A: "I want to hold your hand hand hand hand hand hand hand hand."

☆   ☆   ☆

Q: "What did one casket say to the other casket?"

A: "Is that you, coffin?"

☆   ☆   ☆

Q: "On which side does a chicken have the most feathers?"

A: "The outside."

☆   ☆   ☆

Q: "What's gray on the inside and clear on the outside?"

A: "An elephant in a baggie."

☆   ☆   ☆

Q: "What would you get if you crossed a flea with a rabbit?"

A: "A Bug's Bunny."

☆   ☆   ☆

Q: "Why do cows wear bells?"

A: "Because their horns don't work."

☆   ☆   ☆

Q: "What do you get when you cross a goat and an owl?"

A: "A hootenanny."

☆   ☆   ☆

Q: "What do you get when you cross peanut butter with an elephant?"

A: "You either get peanut butter that never forgets or an elephant that sticks to the roof of your mouth."

☆　☆　☆

Q: "Why do elephants have wrinkles?"

A: "Have you ever tried to iron one?"

☆　☆　☆

Q: "What do they call a bull that sleeps a lot?"

A: "A bulldozer."

☆　☆　☆

Q: "How many dead people are there in a cemetery?"

A: "All of them."

☆　☆　☆

Q: "What did one ear say to the other?"

A: "I didn't know we lived on the same block."

☆　☆　☆

Q: "Why did they make the fingers on the Statue of Liberty only eleven inches long?"

A: "One inch longer and it would have been a foot."

☆　☆　☆

Q: "How do you make anti-freeze?"

A: "Steal her blanket."

☆　☆　☆

Q: "April showers bring May flowers, but what do May flowers bring?"

A: "Pilgrims."

☆　☆　☆

Q: "What does an elephant do when he hurts his toe?"

A: "He calls a tow truck."